Be Free Cooking

The Allergen-Aware Cook

Side-by-side recipes with and without gluten,
wheat, dairy, casein, egg, nut, corn and soy

Written and Photographed by

CHRISTINA GRAY

Foreword by Katie Kelly, RD

BE FREE COOKING©

Published by Bella Luna Studios

ISBN 978-0-9907023-0-6

Printed in the USA

Food Photography and Styling: Christina Gray

Editor-in-Chief: Nancy Andre

Nutritional Content Editor: Katie Kelly, Registered Dietitian

Graphic Design: LeeAnn Nelson, Nelson Design

Be Free Cooking Logo and Illustration: Frank Mina

Foreword Portrait of Christina Gray © Sue Evans Photography, www.PhotographyBySueEvans.com

Back Cover Portrait of Christina Gray © Jeffrey Hosier, www.JeffreyHosier.com

Hair: Lucy Pirogovsky, Hairdresser on Fire

Be Free Cooking

"Free" Tabbouleh Quinoa, page 43

Important Safety Information

The absolute first thing to do when preparing a meal for someone with a food allergy is to have a conversation about the severity of the allergy. Some people have mild allergies while others have major ones. Food allergies run the gamut of severity and it's important to have a clear understanding of dietary needs at the start.

I have cooked for people who are at both ends of the food allergy spectrum and everywhere in between. I have cooked for people who have no food allergies but are curious how gluten-free tastes. I have cooked for people who eat gluten and dairy-free not because they need to, but because they claim it makes them feel better (they have more energy or feel less full) even though they do not have any apparent symptoms of food intolerances. I have also cooked for people who cannot eat certain allergens at all, and if they do, even the slightest little bit, will have a major reaction. I find this to be the case most likely with gluten, eggs, and nuts.

In the case of severe allergies, you need to be especially careful about cross-contamination. When you cross-contaminate food, it means you have exposed your meal to allergens. The most likely source of cross-contamination is your cutting board. Imagine cutting a loaf of wheat bread and then chopping up all your vegetables and a piece of cooked chicken on the same board. The gluten proteins in that wheat bread have just made their way onto the vegetables and chicken, and ultimately into your stomach. For people with mild allergies, that may not pose a threat, but for people with several allergies, that's a huge problem. Clean and dedicated cutting boards, baking stones, dishware, kitchen towels, dish sponges and utensils need to be used to reduce cross-contamination. Please talk over your lunch or dinner plans with your guests and evaluate together what approach you will be taking in the kitchen. Please read my "Tips for Starting Out" section for more helpful hints on reducing the risk of cross-contamination.

In writing this cookbook, I have discovered that not all brands are the same. One brand of tomato sauce may be allergen-free, yet a different brand could contain dairy, casein, corn and/or soy. While I have done my best to label each allergen properly in all "Be" and "Free" recipes, you will need to do your part in reading the labels carefully for each and every ingredient you buy. Even though I claim some recipes are "free" of certain ingredients, you cannot take my word for it because I cannot guarantee the brand of ingredients you buy is truly allergen-free. While I make my best guess that parsley and mandarin oranges, for example, are allergen-free, you should make sure that it truly is by reading the labels carefully. If a label claims "processed in a factory that shares equipment with gluten, wheat, dairy, casein, egg, nut, corn or soy" then you need to decide if that is an acceptable level of allergen exposure for your dining companion. Rule of thumb is always better to be safe than sorry.

Please do not assume a product you bought last week has the same ingredients this week. Companies can change ingredients and you would never know unless you checked the label. Please do not skip this step as label reading is your best and only way to ensure the food you prepare contains only the ingredients you want. This process does not take long and will get easier as you practice. If there is no ingredient label on something, (from a farmers market or fair, for example), play it safe and do not buy it if you need to be allergen-conscious. Again, it is better to be safe than sorry when you are catering to someone with food allergies.

When making a "Be" and a "Free" recipe simultaneously, be sure not to mix one up for the other. Although the whole point of this cookbook was to make recipes feel and taste similar, each recipe is definitely not the same. Take extra care during those times when providing two versions. Make sure that they are clearly labeled and easy to identify. For those dining companions with severe food allergies, please take extra care with labeling so you know exactly what you are eating.

While I have been diligent in proofing this cookbook and having experts proof it as well to ensure the allergen call-outs are accurate, please be sure to double check in the event there is an error. For this cookbook (and any cookbook for that matter), with delicate subject matter such as this, always do your own check for accuracy. There are inherent risks involved when cooking for people with allergies, and given the fact we are all human and imperfect, it makes sense to read and evaluate everything carefully.

*Dedicated with love
to my sister Julie Zan.*

Preface

In October of 2008, a friend brought her 2-year-old son to my home so I could babysit. She put his EpiPen (epinephrine autoinjector in case of anaphylaxis) on the kitchen counter and said he was allergic to gluten, eggs, and nuts. She showed me how to use the EpiPen, made sure I knew how to do it myself, and then said she would be back in two hours. It was at that point I felt like I needed to use the Epi-Pen on myself because I was in shock at the thought of hurting this little boy from something I might feed him. I didn't really even know what gluten was. Is it in an apple? Is it in a graham cracker? My friend said her son wouldn't need to eat because she fed him right before he came over, which was good, because I knew I wasn't going to give him anything but water. That was the day I realized I needed to become educated on gluten and learn all I could about food allergens. Even though I have no food allergies, I felt compelled to learn all I could about them. I know I am not alone on this journey. As of April 2014, 15 million people in the United States had food allergies. That seems like a big number, but the even larger number is the 299 million people who don't. If you are one of those 299 million people without a food allergy and are interested in learning how to cook allergen-free, then *Be Free Cooking* is perfect for you.

I do not claim to be a chef or a doctor. However, I do claim to be a person who cares about my friends and family who have food allergies, and I care enough to share my culinary journey with you. The combination of my love

of cooking, sympathy for those who have food allergies, and need for gathering everyone at the same dinner table to eat a meal is why I decided to write *Be Free Cooking*.

There are two recipe versions in this cookbook: a "Be" and a "Free" version. The "Be" recipe stands for a traditional preparation of a dish that may contain the eight food allergens highlighted in this book: gluten, wheat, dairy, casein, egg, nut, corn, and soy. The "Free" recipe stands for a modified version of the original in which the 8 allergens have been removed. Both versions are shown side-by-side so you can decide which one is appropriate for you or your allergen-sensitive dining companion. Having both recipes, "Be" and "Free" versions, means you just need one single cookbook to meet everyone's food needs.

Be Free Cooking helped me take the fear out of my kitchen and put the fun back into it. This cookbook represents the way I eat. I cook "Be" for my family and myself and cook "Free" for my friends and family who need allergen-safe meals. Having both recipes in one cookbook makes it an easy reference to quickly find the right recipe for any cooking situation.

Please take the time to read the "Tips For Starting Out" section before starting. The two most important things you can do before making any allergen-free meal are to read the labels and have a clean food preparation area. Read every label for every ingredient you buy. Never skip this step! You would be surprised at the allergens in your food that you were not aware of. Always start out with a clean surface to reduce cross-contamination. That means using a dedicated cutting board, baking stone, hand towel, and even sponge to reduce allergen exposure.

Thank you for buying this cookbook and for caring about your friends and family with food allergies. I hope you find this cookbook an easy roadmap for meals that cater to any situation, food allergy or not. Eat Well and Be Free!

Cheers,

Christina

Christina Gray

"Be" Pumpkin Patch Soup, page 2

Foreword

We all probably know someone who has a food allergy or we may have one ourselves. With up to 15 million Americans affected by food allergies, people are starting to think more about what is in their food. This should not be a burden for friends or family; this should be a new way to think about the food you eat and to look at fun new ways to prepare it. Cooking at home allows you to be in control of what goes into your meals and to learn new ways to try different foods and flavors.

Be Free Cooking comes at a time when an increasing number of individuals are becoming more aware of food allergies. Having a cookbook with the dual ability of providing recipes for those who need to remove allergens from their diet while also allowing the same recipe to be altered for those who are not affected by food allergens is extremely beneficial. The uses for this cookbook are endless: it is helpful for those with food allergies, those who have friends or family with allergies, or those who are heading to a BBQ or party at the office where someone has food allergies. Christina took the time creating each unique recipe once she realized there was a need for a cookbook that could help her create tasty foods for her friends and family that they could enjoy without worry.

I have a weekly goal of finding new recipes to try that highlight a different fruit, vegetable or cooking technique. The passion I have for food and nutrition has driven me to pursue a career as a Registered Dietitian. I work at a hospital in Pleasanton, California, where I see a range of patients, many of whom struggle with food allergies. Providing education for this patient population is important. Once they are home and on their own to cook for themselves, it can be difficult to decide what foods are okay to add to their diet and which ones they should omit.

My experience providing nutrition education with a variety of patients has shown me that there is a need for a cookbook for those who struggle with food allergies. I have read through each recipe to verify that the allergens listed are correct. If a food contains or may contain one of the eight allergens, I made sure to carefully list them.

Be mindful of reading ingredient labels when using different packaged items than the ones listed. There may be different allergens in a specific product that may not be in similar products.

Be Free Cooking is two cookbooks in one, and it offers helpful anecdotes and stories of Christina and her charming family. I hope to see more people gain faith in their cooking abilities by trying new recipes. Hopefully you will begin to feel more confident when cooking for a group where food allergens need to be avoided. Christina's passion for food, health, and nutrition, with a balance of great taste, makes this a kitchen must-have. Whenever I bring a *"Be Free Cooking"* recipe to a party, I'm sure to have a request for the recipe!

Katie

Katie Kelly, Registered Dietitian

Introduction

Be Free Cooking is more than a cookbook. *Be Free Cooking* is a cooking approach that simultaneously addresses the two segments of the population—those with food allergies and those without. *Be Free Cooking* will be an invaluable single cooking reference for those people needing to learn how to cook allergen-free. It will also act as your guide for preparing traditional dishes you have come to love.

Be Free Cooking provides a traditional recipe along with that recipe's allergy-friendly counterpart. Be Free Cooking identifies 8 common allergens: gluten, wheat, dairy, casein, egg, nut, corn, and soy. By identifying these allergens individually, this cookbook will serve as a quick roadmap for those needing help understanding allergen-free cooking.

There is a "Be" segment and a "Free" segment to my cooking approach. The "Be" in *Be Free Cooking* represents a traditional way a dish is prepared that often includes these 8 allergens. The "Free" in *Be Free Cooking* is a modified version of traditional recipes in which I have eliminated all of the eight common food allergens.

Showing a "Be" recipe side by side with its "Free" counterpart gives the home chef two versions to prepare because in most cases, just one person at the dinner table has the food allergy. The two dishes, a "Be" and a "Free" version can meet everyone's needs, from both a taste and allergy perspective. The recipe on the left side of the page is the "Be" version while the recipe on the right side of the page is its equally delicious and "Free" counterpart.

The example recipes at left are for pumpkin soup. Depending on who you are serving, you can choose the "Be" version, which is a creamy, cheesy roasted pumpkin soup and contains gluten, wheat, dairy, casein, corn and soy. Alternatively, you could use the "Free" version which is free of all of those allergens and is equally delicious. Serving both soups at a dinner party means you can cater to the food needs of all your guests. Having two recipe versions in the cookbook also means you can just make one, the right one, for the people you are serving.

If you decide to provide a "Be" dish alongside a "Free" one, please read the section titled "Tips For Starting Out" before beginning. This will help you reduce the risk of allergen-contamination and give you some pointers on keeping your work area clean and safe.

Allergy sufferers do not have to walk the road of meal planning and food awareness alone anymore. *Be Free Cooking* demonstrates that you do not need to have a food allergy to understand how to navigate the waters of food choices and preparation.

The left side is a "Be" recipe,
The right side is a "Free" recipe.

Tips For Starting Out

This guide is a resource to get you quickly and easily into the kitchen and cooking an appropriate allergen-safe meal. For some people cross-contamination is not an issue and the worry of having a small amount of allergen exposure poses no risk. Other people with major food allergies have severe reactions when exposed to even the smallest amount of gluten. Be sure to talk with your dining companions to identify their food allergies and needs, and modify your cooking area accordingly. Here are a few tips to make sure there is no accidental cross-contamination and allergen exposure.

READ EVERY LABEL

- Always check every label. Even if you think something does not contain an allergen, it is always worth double-checking. Manufacturers change their product ingredients from time to time, so your cereal that you ate last week could indeed have an ingredient change the next time you buy it.

- If something is wheat-free, that does not mean is it gluten-free. A wheat-free product could have barley, rye, malt, triticale (and more), all of which contain gluten.

- Soy (and soy lecithin) and corn (and high-fructose corn syrup) are common ingredients added to numerous products. Again, check labels carefully if you need to avoid them.

- If the product you are buying has ingredients you are not sure of, do not buy it. Educate yourself on what every ingredient is and what it means before consuming.

- If the product you are buying does not have an ingredients label, don't buy it. It is better to be safe than sorry.

COOKWARE TIPS

Buy a separate cutting board
This is especially important with wooden surfaces that can be nearly impossible to keep clean and can contain allergens within the wood. A separate cutting board will eliminate any cross-contamination. This cutting surface should never be exposed to any of our 8 allergens. To make it easy to identify, mark it clearly with a permanent marker or buy a special color.

Buy separate cooking utensils
Again, if utensils are wooden, it can be hard to rinse away all of the allergen materials that they have touched. Buy separate utensils to be used only with allergen-free food preparation. These utensils should never be exposed to any of our 8 allergens. Again, to make it easy to identify, mark it clearly with a permanent marker or buy a special color.

Buy a separate cleaning sponge
Sponges can absorb allergen particles after cleaning plates and utensils. Just to be safe, have a sponge or other cleaning tool that is dedicated to allergen-free cooking. I cut the corner of the sponge to mark that it is the one for allergen-free cooking. You could also use color to identify.

Use a separate drying cloth
Drying cloths can carry trace amounts of allergens that may be enough to cause cross-contamination. To be on the safe side, always use a clean and specific towel just for allergen-free cooking.

Use common sense
I am sure there are other ways to keep a cooking environment clean. Do your part in evaluating your cooking area for safety and make the necessary changes.

PREPARATION TIPS

Wash your hands
Any time you start an allergen-free recipe (or any recipe really), make sure you wash your hands well. That way you have eliminated any allergen exposure from a previous meal you prepared.

Start clean
A completely clean workspace is essential. If you are making both a "Be" recipe along with a "Free" one, make the "Free" meal first. Be sure to use the cutting boards and utensils dedicated to allergen-free cooking.

A clean grill
If you are barbecuing, be sure the grill is clean and the previous food particles have burned away.

Clean dishes
Be sure all the dishes and eating utensils are thoroughly clean. The best thing is to wash them right before use with the sponge dedicated to allergen-free cooking.

Serve food separately
Never place a "Be" recipe on the same platter as a "Free" recipe. Always use clean and separate serving trays.

Label
If you are serving food at a party, write a quick ingredients list and place it next to the dish. People will be able to quickly see what foods are right for them.

Go organic
Whenever possible, buy organic fruits and vegetables. In the case of meat, always buy grass fed.

I cannot stress enough the importance of reading labels. Even foods that you would think are allergen-free can be a huge source of hidden allergens that can cause harm. Broth, for example, usually contains wheat, corn, and soybean oil depending on the brand. Choose organic stock to reduce the risk of added allergens. Traditional wheat-based bread crumbs commonly contain fillers like corn and soy. Even Italian seasoning blends, or seasoned salt, can contain wheat, soy, and corn. Check all labels carefully.

"Free"

SOUP

PUMPKIN PATCH SOUP

'Be'
Traditional Recipe

SERVES
1-2

TIME REQUIRED
100 min
(20-30 prep + 60-70 cooking)

1 small pie pumpkin (3 lbs)

1 tbsp olive oil to coat outside of pumpkin

1 cup chicken stock, warmed

½ cup heavy cream, warmed

2 tbsp butter

¼ cup cheddar/jack cheese blend

1 tbsp unbleached all-purpose flour

pinch of:
  salt
  black pepper
  cayenne pepper
  garlic powder
  allspice

TIPS

⇒ This recipe does not work as well with larger pumpkins. Stick to the small pie pumpkins for this recipe.

Pumpkin Patch Soup

Preheat oven to 450 degrees.

Cut the top of the pumpkin in a circle, about 1-2 inches around the stem. Clean the inside of the pumpkin of all seeds and fibers. Discard seeds and fibers and save the top.

Place the cleaned pumpkin in a round baking dish (or similar roasting pan). Pour the chicken stock and heavy cream into the pumpkin along with the butter, cheese and flour. Don't fill the pumpkin more an ¾ full or the soup may spill over during cooking. Stir gently.

Add a sprinkle of each (or a heavier amount to suit your taste) of the salt, black pepper, cayenne pepper, garlic powder and allspice.

Cover with the pumpkin top and bake for 60-70 minutes or until the inside flesh of the pumpkin is soft.

Let the pumpkin cool for about 10 minutes or until cool enough to handle. Stir the soup and very gently scrape away the flesh of the pumpkin into the soup. (If you want to serve the soup from the pumpkin, it's a good idea to move the whole pumpkin to a serving tray before scraping the inside walls.)

Be sure not to scrape too hard or to take too much away from the cavity of the pumpkin. You don't want to pierce the skin or cause the pumpkin to collapse. The more pumpkin flesh you add into your soup the thicker it will become. For a smoother consistency, blend the soup before serving.

Eat the soup right out of the pumpkin or transfer the soup to a serving bowl.

HARVEST PUMPKIN SOUP

'Free'
Allergen-free Recipe

SERVES
1-2

TIME REQUIRED
100 min
(20-30 prep + 60-70 cooking)

⊘ GLUTEN
⊘ WHEAT
⊘ DAIRY
⊘ CASEIN
⊘ EGG
⊘ NUT
⊘ CORN
⊘ SOY

Read all food labels carefully and choose only products that are free of unwanted allergens for use in this recipe.

1 small pie pumpkin (3 lbs)

2 tbsp olive oil for sauté

1 shallot, finely minced

1 garlic clove, pressed

½ cup rice milk

8 oz allergen-free vegetable stock

½ tsp arrowroot powder

1 tsp allergen-free pumpkin pie spice (try an organic blend to avoid added sulfites)

2 tbsp sugar

Pinch of: salt, pepper and cayenne pepper

Harvest Pumpkin Soup

Preheat the oven to 450 degrees.

Cut the top of the pumpkin in a circle, about 1-2 inches around the stem. Clean the inside of the pumpkin of all seeds and fibers. Discard seeds and fibers and save the top.

Place the pumpkin into a round baking dish (or similar roasting pan).

Add olive oil to a small sauté pan over medium heat. Cook shallots and garlic until fragrant (about 1-2 minutes) and spoon everything into the pumpkin. The shallots and garlic can burn quickly, so watch carefully.

Add the rest of the ingredients into the pumpkin, filling the pumpkin only about ¾ full to avoid spill-over during cooking. Cover with pumpkin top and bake for 60-70 minutes until the inside pumpkin flesh is tender and soft.

Let the pumpkin cool for about 10 minutes, until cool enough to handle. Stir the soup and very gently scrape away the flesh of the pumpkin into the soup. (If you want to serve the soup from the pumpkin, it's a good idea to move the whole pumpkin to a serving tray before scraping the inside walls.)

Be sure not to scrape too hard or to take too much away from the cavity of the pumpkin. You don't want to pierce the skin or cause the pumpkin to collapse. The more pumpkin flesh you add into your soup the thicker it will become.

If you want a creamier soup, blend it for just a minute on the lowest blender setting. Serve directly from your pumpkin or transfer to a serving bowl.

TIP

⇒ Pumpkins are a very good source of beta carotene/Vitamin A, Vitamin C, potassium, and fiber. Make pumpkin soup a standard menu item in the autumn for a healthy and delicious meal.

3

✓	GLUTEN
✓	WHEAT
✓	DAIRY
✓	CASEIN
⊘	EGG
⊘	NUT
✓	CORN
✓	SOY

'Be'
Traditional
Recipe

SERVES
4-6

TIME REQUIRED
115 min
(25 prep + 90 cooking)

¼ cup olive oil

1 Anaheim chili,
    quartered and seeded

½ red bell pepper

15 baby carrots

½ onion, sliced

1 small zucchini, sliced

64 oz vegetable stock

4 cloves garlic, sliced

1 cup frozen or fresh soybeans

¼ tsp + dash salt

dash Italian seasoning

1 tsp cayenne pepper

½ cup orzo

2 oz Parmesan cheese

Vegetable Soup

Preheat the oven to 400 degrees.

In a heavy casserole dish, add Anaheim chili, bell pepper, carrots, onion, and zucchini. Pour in the oil to coat. Sprinkle with salt and bake for 50 minutes. Turn the vegetables about 3 times during baking to ensure even browning.

In a large stock pot, add the vegetable stock and bring to a boil. When the roasted vegetables are done, remove them from the oven and add to the stock. Then add the sliced garlic, soybeans, ¼ tsp salt, Italian seasoning and cayenne pepper. Stir and let simmer for 10-20 minutes.

Remove from heat and transfer the hot soup to a separate large bowl. Ladle 2 cups at a time into a blender and blend until smooth (about 30 seconds). Repeat until all the soup has been blended. An immersion blender would be great to use if you have one.

Transfer back into the large stock pot, cup by cup, after it is blended. Once all the soup has been blended and added to the pot, bring it back to a boil.

Add ½ cup orzo and cook according to package instructions. Once the orzo is cooked, the soup is done and ready to eat. Garnish with Parmesan cheese and enjoy.

Mangia!

TIP

⇒ You don't have to blend this soup, but I love the flavor this way. You could also choose to blend only half to give your soup a chunkier texture.

4

'Free'
Allergen-free Recipe

SERVES
3-4

TIME REQUIRED
90 min
(30 prep + 60 cooking)

⊘ GLUTEN
⊘ WHEAT
⊘ DAIRY
⊘ CASEIN
⊘ EGG
⊘ NUT
⊘ CORN
⊘ SOY

Read all food labels carefully and choose only products that are free of unwanted allergens for use in this recipe.

64 oz organic, allergen-free vegetable stock

6 tbsp olive oil for sautéing, divided into thirds

2 carrots, chopped

½ red bell pepper, chopped

½ green bell pepper, chopped

½ orange bell pepper, chopped

½ Anaheim chili, diced

½ medium size yellow onion, chopped

2 cloves garlic, minced

½ tsp salt

1 celery stalk, chopped

Four Pepper Soup

Pour the vegetable stock into a large pot and bring to a boil. Reduce to low.

Add 2 tablespoons of the olive oil to a sauté pan. Bring to medium heat and then add carrots. Stir the carrots so they brown evenly in the oil. Once they start to brown slightly, remove from heat and place directly into the warm vegetable stock.

Repeat the steps above with the red, green and orange bell peppers and the Anaheim chili. Once browned slightly, remove from heat and add to stock.

Repeat the steps above with the onion. Just before the onions look like they are going to start browning, add the garlic. Garlic burns fast, so just a short time in the pan releases the flavor you need. Add salt. Once the onions and garlic start to brown, remove from heat and add to stock.

Add the celery directly into the stock.

Turn the heat up to medium and gently simmer for about 20 minutes.

Taste your soup. The longer it simmers the more robust the flavor will become. If you like it now, then take it away from the heat and serve. If you want more flavor, turn the heat to low and leave it for a while longer. The liquid will evaporate more as time passes and will make the soup more dense. It will also reduce the serving size.

TIP
⇒ Use the leftover bell peppers in a stir fry, to scoop up some tasty hummus, or just eat them plain. They are delicious raw and so good for you too!

DECADENT POTATO SOUP

✓	GLUTEN
✓	WHEAT
✓	DAIRY
✓	CASEIN
⊘	EGG
⊘	NUT
✓	CORN
✓	SOY

'Be'
Traditional
Recipe

SERVES
2-3

TIME REQUIRED
45 min
(15 prep + 30 cooking)

2 large Yukon gold potatoes

4 cloves garlic, peeled

4 slices of bacon,
    cooked and crumbled

2 tbsp butter

1 large yellow onion, chopped

32 oz chicken stock

½ cup heavy cream

1 cup shredded cheddar/jack
    blend cheese

TIPS

⇒ My dear friend Carri loves this dish. She says it's her go-to-winter-day soup. I say it's a go-to-any-day soup! One spoonful and you'll see why.

⇒ It also makes a great appetizer at parties. Serve in small shot glasses and you have a show stopper of a starter!

Decadent Potato Soup

Peel and cube the potatoes. Fill a large stock pot with water and bring to a boil. Add the cubed potatoes and whole garlic cloves to the boiling water.

Boil the potatoes until they are tender and break apart when pierced with a fork, about 10-15 minutes.

While potatoes are boiling, brown the bacon in a medium stock pot. Remove bacon from heat once cooked and crumble when cool. Set bacon aside.

In the bacon drippings, add butter and chopped onion and sauté on low heat for about 10 minutes. Cook the onions until they are translucent, being careful not to let them brown.

Add the chicken stock to the sautéed onions and bring to a gentle boil.

Once the potatoes are done cooking, drain them and put them back into the same pot. Mash together the cooked garlic and potatoes.

One ladle at a time, add the stock to the potato mixture. Continue until all the stock has been added.

Add the cream and cheese. Blend the mixture in small batches to make it smooth. You could also blend only half the mixture if you like more texture.

Sprinkle crumbled bacon on top, along with more shredded cheese and serve.

6

BAKED POTATO SOUP

'Free'
Allergen-free Recipe

⊘	GLUTEN
⊘	WHEAT
⊘	DAIRY
⊘	CASEIN
⊘	EGG
⊘	NUT
⊘	CORN
⊘	SOY

SERVES
3-4

TIME REQUIRED
90 min
(30 prep + 60 cooking)

Read all food labels carefully and choose only products that are free of unwanted allergens for use in this recipe.

2 large Yukon gold potatoes

6 garlic cloves

5 tbsp olive oil, divided:
    1 tbsp for baking garlic
    4 tbsp for sauté

salt and pepper to taste

4 strips of bacon

2 green onions, chopped and divided

24 oz organic, allergen-free chicken or vegetable stock

½ tsp paprika

1 green onion, chopped

Baked Potato Soup

Pre-heat the oven to 400 degrees.

Wash the potatoes well and pat dry. Do not peel. Bake until soft, about 40-60 minutes.

Wrap garlic cloves along with 1 tbsp of olive oil in aluminum foil. Bake the garlic in the oven during the last 20 minutes of baking time.

While potatoes are baking, brown bacon in a medium stock pot. Remove bacon from heat once cooked and crumble when cool. Set bacon aside.

In the bacon drippings, add 4 tbsp olive oil. Once hot, add half of the chopped green onions and sauté on low heat for 10 minutes. Add the stock to the green onions and bring to a gentle boil.

Once the potatoes and garlic are done cooking, remove and set aside. You can peel the potatoes or keep the skin on. If you want to peel them, let them cool for a few minutes so the skin is easier to remove. In a large pot or bowl, mash together the cooked garlic and potatoes. Add paprika.

One ladle at a time, add the stock mixture to the potato mixture and mash well. Continue until all the stock has been added or until desired consistency. Blend all or half of the soup for a creamy texture.

Sprinkle the crumbled bacon and remaining green onions on top and serve.

TIP

⇒ To add some flavor complexity to this soup, add chopped ham, diced bell peppers, jalapeños, or anything else you like. Make this soup your own by adding extra ingredients you love.

www.befreecooking.blogspot.com   *To reduce cross-contamination use cutting boards, towels, utensils, and dish sponges dedicated for allergen-free cooking.*

7

HEARTY TORTILLA SOUP

'Be'
Traditional Recipe

SERVES
4-6

TIME REQUIRED
60 min
(20 prep + 40 cooking)

✓	GLUTEN
✓	WHEAT
✓	DAIRY
✓	CASEIN
⊘	EGG
⊘	NUT
✓	CORN
✓	SOY

¼ cup + 1 tbsp light olive oil, divided:
 ¼ cup for sauté
 1 tbsp for tortilla strips

1 medium onion, chopped

2 cloves garlic, chopped

salt

2 tomatoes, chopped

14.5 oz can crushed tomatoes,
 including liquid

64 oz chicken stock

½ tsp cumin

1 small roasted pasilla pepper, seeded
 and chopped

2 cups rotisserie chicken, shredded

3 flour tortillas

2 avocados

3 tbsp cilantro to garnish

½ cup cotija cheese as topping

TIP

⇒ I love the flavor that develops when roasting peppers, but this step is optional. If you want more heat, roast a jalapeño instead.

Hearty Tortilla Soup

In a stock pot, add ¼ cup light olive oil and bring to medium heat.
Add half of the onions and sauté for a few minutes. Add garlic and continue to sauté until the garlic and the onions start to turn very light brown.
Add salt to boost flavor.

Add the fresh, chopped tomatoes and sauté for a few more minutes.
Add the can of crushed tomatoes and bring to a slight boil. Once it starts to boil, add the chicken stock and cumin. Stir all ingredients together and keep the heat just high enough for the soup to boil lightly.

While the soup is cooking, preheat the barbecue. Place your pasilla pepper on the grill on high heat. Rotate the pepper four times after each section burns and the skin is roasted. Place the pepper in a paper bag for about 5 minutes. Peel away the burned and bubbled skin and cut it in half. Discard the seeds and chop well.

Add the chopped, roasted pepper to the soup along with the shredded chicken and the remaining onion. Allow soup to simmer 5-10 more minutes.

For the tortilla strips, brush a layer of oil on one side of the tortilla and sprinkle with salt. Cut the tortilla in half, putting one onto the other. Cut long 1 inch strips all the way across. Place on a baking stone. Bake at 450 degrees for 5-10 minutes. Watch closely; they can burn quickly!

When serving, place a few avocado slices on the top of the soup along with a bit of cilantro and cotija cheese. Either top the soup with the tortilla strips or serve on the side.

8

CHICKEN TORTILLA SOUP

⊘	GLUTEN
⊘	WHEAT
⊘	DAIRY
⊘	CASEIN
⊘	EGG
⊘	NUT
⊘	CORN
⊘	SOY

'Free'
Allergen-free Recipe

SERVES
4-6

TIME REQUIRED
90 min
(15 prep + 60-120 cooking)

Read all food labels carefully and choose only products that are free of unwanted allergens for use in this recipe.

MARINADE

2 tbsp lemon juice

4 tbsp olive oil

3 cloves garlic, pressed

½ tsp each cumin and paprika

½ tsp salt

SOUP

2 organic chicken breasts

4 tbsp olive oil

¾ cup each carrot, celery, green bell pepper and onion, chopped

3 cloves garlic, chopped

¼ cup cilantro, chopped

salt and pepper

64 oz organic, allergen-free chicken stock

14 oz can chopped tomatoes, with liquid

14 oz can black beans, drained

1 avocado, sliced

Chicken Tortilla Soup

Preheat oven to 400 degrees.

Combine all of the marinade ingredients and mix well. Place chicken breasts in a baking dish and cover with the marinade, coating both sides of the chicken. Bake, uncovered, about 30 minutes or until fully cooked.

In a large stock pot, bring olive oil to medium heat. Add carrots, celery, green bell pepper, onions and garlic and sauté until tender. Add cilantro and salt and pepper to taste.

Add the stock, tomatoes and black beans to the stock pot and bring to a slight boil. Reduce heat to medium-low and simmer, covered, for at least 1 hour.
If you have time, simmer for up to 3 hours. The longer cooking time allows more flavor to develop.

Shred or chop the chicken once it is finished cooking. Add to the soup during the last 20 minutes of cooking. Be sure to add in all the juices from the pan for extra flavor.

Top with avocado slices and serve.

(You can make this soup in the crock pot, too! Just add all of the ingredients, including the marinade, and let it cook for 6-8 hours on low.)

9

To reduce cross-contamination use cutting boards, towels, utensils, and dish sponges dedicated for allergen-free cooking.

SPLIT PEA SOUP

✓	GLUTEN
✓	WHEAT
✓	DAIRY
✓	CASEIN
✓	EGG
⊘	NUT
✓	CORN
✓	SOY

'Be'
Traditional
Recipe

SERVES
4-5

TIME REQUIRED
8-9 hrs
(15 min prep +
8-9 hrs cooking)

7 cups water

16 oz dried split peas,
not soaked

1.5 lbs ham shank or ham hocks

15 baby carrots, chopped

½ can (5 oz) cream of celery
soup

3 garlic cloves, chopped

1 bay leaf

4 oz diced green chilies

1 small potato, diced small

½ white onion, chopped

saltine crackers, optional

Split Pea Soup

Turn your crock pot on the low setting and pour in water.

Add all of the remaining ingredients and cook for 8-9 hours.

Take out the ham hock and remove the fat and bones.

Shred the meat and put it back into the soup.

Remove the bay leaf before serving.

Serve hot with saltine crackers.

(If you want to make this recipe gluten-free, skip the saltine crackers and be sure to check the label on the celery soup for gluten.)

TIP

⇒ This soup is awesome! I am not sure what I love more - that it's super easy to make or that it tastes so incredible. This is an amazing winter soup or a perfect dinner for a busy family. I get this going in the morning and dinner is ready, hot and delicious after everyone is home from school and work.

10

'Free'

Allergen-free
Recipe

SERVES

2-3

TIME REQUIRED

30 min

(10 prep + 20 cooking)

⊘ GLUTEN

⊘ WHEAT

⊘ DAIRY

⊘ CASEIN

⊘ EGG

⊘ NUT

⊘ CORN

⊘ SOY

Read all food labels carefully and choose only products that are free of unwanted allergens for use in this recipe.

4 tbsp olive oil

1 small yellow onion, chopped

4 cloves garlic, chopped

dash red pepper flakes

16 oz frozen or fresh peas

14 oz organic, allergen-free
   vegetable stock

dash allergen-free
   Herbs de Provence

¼ tsp salt

Fresh Pea Soup

In a large stock pot, heat the olive oil over medium heat. Add chopped onions, garlic and red pepper flakes and sauté until the onions become translucent and the garlic becomes fragrant.

Add fresh or frozen peas and stir gently until the peas start to thaw and soften.

Add vegetable stock, Herbs de Provence and salt.

(If you don't have a shaker of Herbs de Provence on hand, look to your spice rack for rosemary, marjoram, thyme, and lavender and add a dash of each—or more—to taste.)

Bring to a boil and then reduce heat to low.

Cook covered for 10-15 more minutes.

Blend the soup in batches and serve warm.

TIP

⇒ Don't think you're a pea soup fan? This recipe might make you reconsider. Not only is it easy, tasty and inexpensive, it's incredibly healthy, too! Peas are a great source of antioxidants and have anti-inflammatory benefits.

CHICKEN ORZO SOUP

'Be'
Traditional Recipe

SERVES
8

TIME REQUIRED
8¼ hrs
(15 min prep + 8 hrs cooking)

5-6 lb whole chicken

2 tsp salt

2 tsp black pepper

8 oz can diced green chilies

3 garlic cloves, chopped

1½ cups each celery, onion and carrot, chopped

6 cups water

½ cup orzo (uncooked)

8 tbsp shredded Parmesan cheese

TIPS

⇒ When you take the chicken out of the crock pot, be careful - it will be so tender it will most likely fall apart as you lift it out. Gently go through the chicken and carefully remove all the bones. Some are tiny!

⇒ This recipe is so easy! Get it going in the morning and when you come home in the evening, you have awesome homemade soup that the whole family will love.

Chicken Orzo Soup

Rinse the chicken well and remove and discard any extra meat in the cavity of the bird.

Place the cleaned chicken into the crock pot. Season the entire chicken with salt and pepper.

Add green chilies, chopped garlic, celery, carrots and onions.

Add 6 cups of water.

Set the crock pot on the low setting and cook for 8 hours, turning the chicken at least once during the cooking time.

Take the chicken from the crock pot. Remove all the meat from the chicken and discard the skin and bones. Add only the meat back into the crock pot.

Add the orzo 30 minutes before you are ready to serve.

Top each serving with Parmesan cheese and enjoy!

'Free'
Allergen-free Recipe

⊘ GLUTEN
⊘ WHEAT
⊘ DAIRY
⊘ CASEIN
⊘ EGG
⊘ NUT
⊘ CORN
⊘ SOY

SERVES
2-3

TIME REQUIRED
8¾ hrs
(20 min prep + 8 hrs, 25 min cooking)

Read all food labels carefully and choose only products that are free of unwanted allergens for use in this recipe.

STOCK

1½ lbs skinless, boneless, organic chicken thighs

9 cups water

4 cloves whole garlic

3 celery stalks, roughly chopped

1 large yellow onion, halved

3 carrots, roughly chopped

1 bay leaf

¼ tsp salt

SOUP

2 tbsp olive oil

1 medium yellow onion, chopped

2 carrots, chopped

2 stalks celery, chopped

9 cups homemade stock

8 oz brown rice pasta

1 tsp salt

black and/or cayenne pepper, to taste

lemon juice, optional

Chicken Noodle Soup

STOCK: In a crock pot, combine chicken, water, garlic, celery, onion, carrots, bay leaf and salt. Cook on low for 6–8 hours or until chicken is completely cooked and very tender.

Put a large strainer into a large bowl and pour all of the crock pot ingredients into the strainer. Separate out the chicken and set aside. Discard the vegetables and bay leaf. The reserved liquid is now your stock.

(You're wondering, "Do I really need to make the stock from scratch?" The answer is yes. One taste of this soup and you'll know why. Canned stock, while fast and easy, will never have the same flavor as homemade. Don't be intimidated by homemade stock. The crock pot does all the hard work and you get all the credit.)

SOUP: In a large pot, add olive oil over medium heat. Add chopped onions, carrots and celery. Sauté for 15 minutes, stirring frequently.

Add the stock and bring to a boil. Add the pasta and cook according to package instructions.

About 2 minutes before the pasta is done, add the chicken meat into the pot along with salt and pepper to taste. Add the optional lemon juice for a bit of brightness. Serve and enjoy.

✓	GLUTEN
✓	WHEAT
✓	DAIRY
✓	CASEIN
⊘	EGG
⊘	NUT
✓	CORN
✓	SOY

JAZZY LENTIL SOUP

'Be'
Traditional Recipe

SERVES
4

TIME REQUIRED
80 min
(20 prep + 60 cooking)

3 bacon slices

2 tbsp butter

½ yellow onion, chopped

10 baby carrots, chopped

4 celery stalks, chopped

3 garlic cloves, chopped

10 oz frozen okra, sliced

1½ cups frozen corn

1 tsp salt

32 oz (4 cups) chicken stock

32 oz (4 cups) water

½ lb lentils, rinsed and sorted

1 tsp fresh rosemary, chopped

1 tsp cayenne pepper

4 small bread rounds

TIP

⇒ I like to substitute fire-roasted corn on the cob for frozen corn in this dish. It gives it great flavor. Just take 2 ears of corn and barbecue them, in the husk, on medium for about 10 minutes. So worth it!

Jazzy Lentil Soup

In a large stock pot, brown the bacon over medium heat.

Remove the bacon and set aside. Crumble the bacon once it cools.

Add butter to the rendered fat in the pot. Once the butter melts, add the onions, carrots, celery, garlic, okra and corn. Add salt. Sauté over medium heat for about 5 minutes, but do not brown.

(I can hear you grumbling about adding butter to bacon fat to sauté the vegetables. But remember, we only cooked 3 slices of bacon and there just isn't enough flavor there alone to make this soup stand out. Adding the butter adds one dimension of flavor that you don't want to skip. Trust me, it will be worth it. You are going to exercise anyway today, right?)

Add chicken stock and water and bring to a boil.

Add lentils, browned bacon and rosemary.

Cook covered over medium heat for 45-55 minutes or until the lentils are totally cooked.

Add cayenne pepper to taste.

Cut the top off of a small bread round. Hollow out the inside and fill with the soup.

(If you want to make this gluten-free, skip the bread rounds and be sure to use organic, allergen-free chicken stock.)

HAM AND LENTIL SOUP

'Free'
Allergen-free Recipe

SERVES
4

TIME REQUIRED
70 min
(10 prep + 45-60 cooking)

⊘ GLUTEN
⊘ WHEAT
⊘ DAIRY
⊘ CASEIN
⊘ EGG
⊘ NUT
⊘ CORN
⊘ SOY

Ham and Lentil Soup

In a stock pot, add olive oil and bring to medium heat.

Add the onion, celery and garlic and sauté until tender.

Add the stock, lentils and ham and cook as directed on the lentil package. Cover partially with a lid.

Once the lentils are cooked to your desired tenderness, add salt and pepper to taste, remove from heat and serve. (*The cooked ham probably has lots of salt in it already, so be sure to taste the soup before you salt it further.*)

Read all food labels carefully and choose only products that are free of unwanted allergens for use in this recipe.

4 tbsp olive oil

1 small onion, chopped

2 stalks celery, chopped

2 cloves garlic, chopped

40-50 oz organic, allergen-free chicken stock

1½ cups lentils

4 oz sliced, extra lean cooked allergen-free ham, chopped or cubed

salt and pepper, to taste

TIPS

⇒ I just love recipes with minimal ingredients. What I love even more are recipes in which the only real steps are to chop and combine. For anyone wanting an easy soup recipe to start with, this one is it.

⇒ Want a bolder flavor? Add Herbs de Provence, Italian Seasoning, cayenne or red pepper flakes near the end of the cooking time.

To reduce cross-contamination use cutting boards, towels, utensils, and dish sponges dedicated for allergen-free cooking.

✓	GLUTEN
✓	WHEAT
✓	DAIRY
✓	CASEIN
⊘	EGG
⊘	NUT
✓	CORN
✓	SOY

CLASSIC ASPARAGUS SOUP

'Be'
Traditional
Recipe

SERVES
6

TIME REQUIRED
40 min
(10 prep + 30 cooking)

1 lb. asparagus

48 oz (6 cups) chicken stock

2 tbsp olive oil

2 tbsp butter

1 yellow onion, chopped

2 cloves garlic, pressed

1 tsp salt

2 tbsp flour

¼ cup heavy cream

1 tsp cayenne pepper

TIP

⇨ I know what some of you are thinking... this recipe uses a blender, so maybe I won't make it. Please don't let that stop you. The best, creamiest soups are made this way, so get out the equipment and just leave it on your counter. Blend just a few soups and you'll be a pro. An immersion blender would make blending even easier if you have one.

Classic Asparagus Soup

Chop an inch off the top tip of each asparagus stem and reserve. Chop an inch off the bottom ends and discard. Chop the rest of the asparagus and set aside.

In a small pot, add 1 cup of chicken stock and bring to a boil. Add the tips of the asparagus and bring to a boil. Cook for just 2-3 minutes to blanch. Remove asparagus tips and rinse under cold water. Reserve the cooking stock.

In a large stock pot, add olive oil and butter over medium heat. Once warm and butter is melted, add onion, chopped asparagus, garlic and salt. Sauté for 5 minutes, but do not brown.

Add the reserved stock to the remaining chicken stock and bring to a soft boil for about 15 minutes, uncovered.

For a smoother consistency, blend the mixture. Add a few ladles at a time to a blender and blend for a few seconds. Add the blended mixture back to the pot and bring to a boil.

Add flour to heavy cream and whisk together. Add this mixture to the pot. Cook for about 5 more minutes for all the ingredients to come together.

Ladle soup into serving bowls, top with a few of the blanched asparagus tips, and sprinkle with cayenne pepper.

16

'Free'
Allergen-free Recipe

SERVES
4

TIME REQUIRED
40 min
(20 prep + 20 cooking)

⊘	GLUTEN
⊘	WHEAT
⊘	DAIRY
⊘	CASEIN
⊘	EGG
⊘	NUT
⊘	CORN
⊘	SOY

Read all food labels carefully and choose only products that are free of unwanted allergens for use in this recipe.

1½ lbs gold potatoes, cubed, skin on

1 lb asparagus, chopped

3 tbsp olive oil

1 small onion, chopped

3 garlic cloves, chopped

4 cups of organic, allergen-free vegetable or chicken stock

2 cups water

1 tsp salt, to taste

pepper to taste

Easy Asparagus Soup

Clean the potatoes and asparagus well. Cut the ends off the asparagus and discard. Chop the asparagus and cut the potatoes into small cubes.

In a large stock pot, heat the olive oil. Add chopped onions and garlic and sauté until the onions become translucent and the garlic becomes fragrant.

Add the stock and water and bring to a boil. Add the potatoes and cook for about 10 minutes, or until the potatoes are half cooked.

Add the chopped asparagus and stir well. Add salt and pepper to taste, and then boil over medium high heat until the potatoes are completely cooked.

Blend the mixture in batches and serve warm.

TIPS

⇒ This soup freezes well, so double or triple the recipe to get ready for winter or even the work week.

⇒ If you have any left over vegetables from the night before, this is a great soup to use them in. Add some of your favorite spices, too, like cayenne or red pepper, or even jalapeños if you'd like to add some heat.

To reduce cross-contamination use cutting boards, towels, utensils, and dish sponges dedicated for allergen-free cooking.

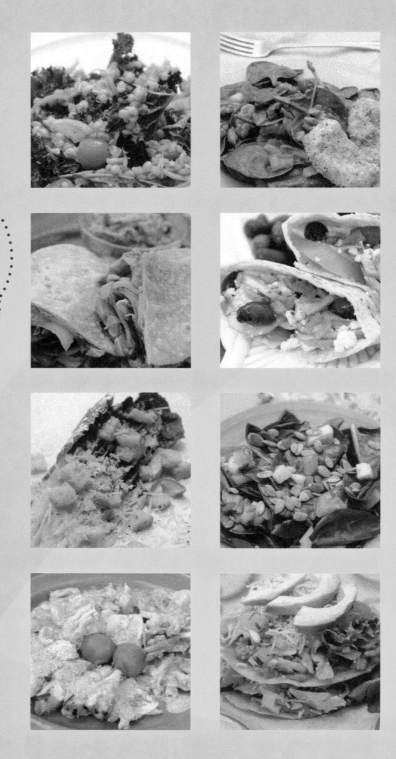

BARLEY KALE SALAD

'Be'
Traditional Recipe

SERVES
4

TIME REQUIRED
50 min
(10 prep + 40 cooking)

Barley Kale Salad

Rinse and cook the barley according to package instructions, usually about 40 minutes.

DRESSING: Add the olive oil, red onions, tomatoes, red wine vinegar, balsamic vinegar, salt, pepper and sugar to a large mixing bowl. Mix well and set aside.

Rinse the kale well. Remove stems and rip leaves into small, bite-sized pieces. Add the kale to the dressing and mix well.

Once the barley is done cooking, rinse with cold water in a colander. Add to the bowl of kale and dressing and mix well to incorporate all the ingredients together.

MAIN DISH

½ cup pearl barley

1 small bunch kale, de-stemmed

DRESSING

¼ cup olive oil

¾ cup red onion, sliced

5 oz grape tomatoes, halved

3 tbsp red wine vinegar

2 tbsp balsamic vinegar

¼ tsp salt

¼ tsp black pepper

1 tsp sugar

TIPS

⇒ This salad is not only good for you, it's filling and delicious, too! The bold flavor and sturdy texture of the barley will wow even the pickiest salad eaters.

⇒ This salad is a perfect choice for a summer picnic (but still should not be left out for more than four hours).

'Free'
Allergen-free Recipe

SERVES
4

TIME REQUIRED
50 min
(10 prep + 50 cooking)

⊘ GLUTEN
⊘ WHEAT
⊘ DAIRY
⊘ CASEIN
⊘ EGG
⊘ NUT
⊘ CORN
⊘ SOY

Read all food labels carefully and choose only products that are free of unwanted allergens for use in this recipe.

MAIN DISH

½ cup quinoa

1 small bunch kale, de-stemmed

½ cup green onion, sliced

½ cup radish, chopped

1 avocado, cubed

DRESSING

5 tbsp olive oil

5 tbsp fresh lemon juice

½ tsp salt

½ tsp pepper

Quinoa Kale Salad

Bring 2 cups of water to a boil in a pot. Add quinoa, reduce heat to low, and cook according to package directions.

DRESSING: Add the olive oil, lemon juice, salt and pepper into a container with a lid. Mix well and set aside.

Rinse the kale well. Remove stems and rip leaves into small bite-sized pieces.

In a large bowl, add the kale, green onion, radish, and avocado. Add the dressing and mix well.

Once the quinoa is done cooking, let it cool for 5 minutes. Once cool, add the quinoa to the bowl of dressed kale and mix well to incorporate all the ingredients together.

TIPS

⇒ I love the spicy bite of radish with the creamy texture of avocado. If you don't like radish, substitute cherry tomatoes or jicama.

⇒ I always make extra dressing to store in the fridge for the next day. I love this salad dressing on top of chicken and steak to add a little flavor boost.

WALNUT SPINACH SALAD

'Be'
Traditional
Recipe

SERVES
2

TIME REQUIRED
30 min
(20 prep + 10 cooking)

MAIN DISH

4 oz goat cheese log

3 tbsp Italian bread crumbs

½ tbsp butter

1 tsp brown sugar

½ cup walnuts

4 oz fresh spinach

2 tbsp red onion, chopped

DRESSING

¼ cup olive oil

4 tbsp balsamic vinegar

1 clove garlic, chopped

1 tbsp lemon juice

1 tbsp water

1 tsp sugar

¼ tsp salt

TIP

⇒ Walnuts and goat cheese are two of my favorite additions to a salad. The creaminess of the goat cheese and the crunch of the walnut, make for one dynamic duo. If you don't have time to bake the goat cheese, just crumble it on top.

Walnut Spinach Salad

Preheat the oven to 400°F.

Cut the goat cheese into 4 pieces. Place bread crumbs on a plate and lightly press goat cheese into crumbs until evenly coated.
Bake for 5 minutes.

In a small sauté pan, melt butter over medium heat. Add brown sugar and stir well.

Once the sugar and butter are combined, add walnuts. Stir until the walnuts are coated and warm. This takes about 5 minutes.
Remove from heat and set aside.

DRESSING: Add olive oil, balsamic vinegar, garlic, lemon juice, water, sugar and salt into a blender. Pulse for about 1 minute until all the ingredients have come together. If the dressing is too thick, add an additional tablespoon of water. *(Don't want to break out the blender? Mix the dressing ingredients in a container with a lid and shake well. The dressing will not be as thick and might separate, but will still taste great.)*

To assemble the salad, combine spinach, candied walnuts and red onion in a large bowl. Add the dressing and mix well.

To plate, add half of your dressed spinach, along with 2 slices of the baked goat cheese. Repeat with second portion and serve.

'Free'
Allergen-free Recipe

SERVES
2

TIME REQUIRED
28 min
(20 prep + 8 cooking)

⊘ GLUTEN
⊘ WHEAT
⊘ DAIRY
⊘ CASEIN
⊘ EGG
⊘ NUT
⊘ CORN
⊘ SOY

Read all food labels carefully and choose only products that are free of unwanted allergens for use in this recipe.

MAIN DISH

3 bacon slices

½ cup green apple, shaved

1 tsp lemon juice

4 oz fresh spinach

2 tbsp dried cranberries

2 tbsp pumpkin seeds

DRESSING

¼ cup olive oil

3 tbsp apple cider vinegar

1 tbsp lemon juice

½ tsp sugar

¼ tsp salt

¼ tsp pepper

Apple Spinach Salad

Cook bacon in a sauté pan over medium heat until crisp. Drain grease and set bacon aside to cool. Crumble once cool.

Shave the skin off a green apple and discard. Begin shaving the flesh of the apple until you have ½ cup. Toss with lemon juice to prevent the apple shavings from browning.

DRESSING: Add olive oil, apple cider vinegar, lemon juice, sugar, salt and pepper to a small container with a lid. Shake well to combine.

Assemble the salad by combining spinach, dried cranberries and pumpkin seeds in a large bowl. Add the dressing and mix well.

To plate, add half of your dressed salad, along with half of the bacon. Spread the shaved apple around the plate.

Repeat with second portion and serve.

TIP

⇨ The dried cranberry, along with the delicate shavings of apple, make this salad delicious. I love adding pumpkin seeds to provide a great crunch.

STUFFED CHICKEN WRAP

'Be'
Traditional Recipe

SERVES
2

TIME REQUIRED
5 min
(5 prep + 0 cooking)

2 tbsp ranch dressing

cayenne pepper

2 spinach tortillas

½ cup rotisserie chicken

6 tbsp french fried onions

½ cup lettuce, julienned

1 tomato, julienned

4 tbsp cheddar/jack blend cheese

4 tbsp BBQ sauce

TIPS

⇒ Supermarket rotisserie chicken can be your best friend. Quick, inexpensive and flavorful, it doesn't get better than that!

⇒ If you are wondering what a french fried onion is, it is an onion that has been battered and fried. You can usually find packaged french fried onions at a local supermarket.

⇒ This recipe requires no cooking! It's delicious, it's easy, and it's almost instant!

Stuffed Chicken Wrap

In a small bowl, add the ranch dressing and enough cayenne pepper to suit your taste. Mix well.

Lay out one tortilla and spread half of the ranch-cayenne dressing over it.

Add half of the chicken, fried onion, lettuce, tomato and cheese.

Drizzle half of the BBQ sauce over the ingredients.

It's not going to be easy to wrap it all up, but do your best. Think of it like a present, close both ends, then wrap from one side to the other.

Repeat with the second tortilla. Cut each wrap in half, if desired, and serve.

'Free'
Allergen-free
Recipe

⊘	GLUTEN
⊘	WHEAT
⊘	DAIRY
⊘	CASEIN
⊘	EGG
⊘	NUT
⊘	CORN
⊘	SOY

SERVES
2

TIME REQUIRED
15 min
(10 prep + 5 cooking)

Read all food labels carefully and choose only products that are free of unwanted allergens for use in this recipe.

MAIN DISH

1 tbsp olive oil

½ small yellow onion, sliced

salt and pepper, to taste

2 allergen-free brown rice tortillas

4 slices oven roasted, organic allergen-free turkey

1 cup spinach leaves

DRESSING

1 ripe avocado

2 tbsp fresh lemon juice

dashes salt and black pepper

Avocado Turkey Wrap

In a pan over medium heat, add olive oil. Add onions, salt and pepper and sauté for about 5 minutes or until the onions become limp and slightly brown. Set aside.

DRESSING: Combine avocado, lemon juice, salt and pepper in a small bowl. Using a fork, press the avocado until it becomes spreadable.

To assemble, spread half of the avocado dressing on a brown rice tortilla. Add half of the grilled onions, 2 slices of turkey, and ½ cup of the spinach leaves. Roll together to close.

Repeat with the second tortilla. Cut each wrap in half, if desired, and serve.

TIPS

⇒ Avocado is a great addition to any sandwich or wrap for those people who love creamy dressings but can't tolerate dairy.

⇒ Brown rice tortillas can be dry and hard to handle, breaking easily when you roll them. To prevent this, try placing the tortilla between two damp paper towerls for a few minutes before rolling.

✓	GLUTEN
✓	WHEAT
✓	DAIRY
✓	CASEIN
✓	EGG
⊘	NUT
✓	CORN
✓	SOY

GREEK PITA WRAP

'Be'
Traditional
Recipe

SERVES
2

TIME REQUIRED
15 min
(15 prep + 0 cooking)

MAIN DISH

2 medium tomatoes, sliced

1 cucumber, peeled, sliced

5 oz pitted kalamata olives

4 oz feta cheese

2 whole pita rounds, halved

DRESSING

¼ cup olive oil

4 tbsp red wine vinegar

¼ tsp dried oregano

½ cup chopped red onion

dash of salt

dash of pepper

Greek Pita Wrap

DRESSING: Combine the olive oil, red wine vinegar, dried oregano, red onion, salt and pepper in a covered container. Shake well.

In a mixing bowl, combine the tomatoes, cucumber, olives and feta cheese and mix well. Add the dressing and stir well to incorporate.

Cut the pita rounds in half. Stuff each half with the tomato/cucumber mixture. Serve immediately.

TIP

⇒ This dish is so fresh and delicious! And the red onion makes it beautiful, as well. It's surprisingly filling and takes only minutes to prepare. This is a fantastic dish for a quick, easy and healthy meal.

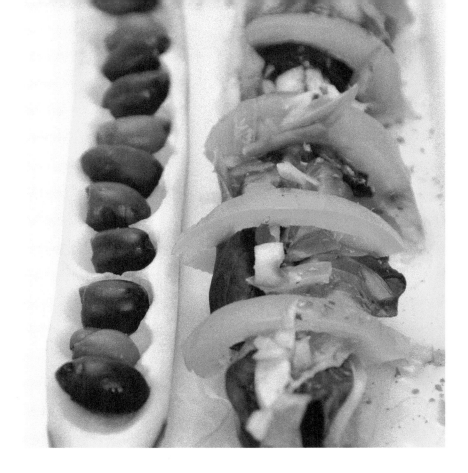

'Free'
Allergen-free
Recipe

SERVES
2

TIME REQUIRED
15 min
(15 prep + 0 cooking)

⊘ GLUTEN
⊘ WHEAT
⊘ DAIRY
⊘ CASEIN
⊘ EGG
⊘ NUT
⊘ CORN
⊘ SOY

Read all food labels carefully and choose only products that are free of unwanted allergens for use in this recipe.

MAIN DISH

2 cucumbers,
    peeled and sliced lengthwise

10 oz pitted kalamata olives

1 cup red leaf lettuce

2 medium tomatoes, sliced

DRESSING

¼ cup olive oil

4 tbsp red wine vinegar

¼ tsp dried oregano

½ cup chopped red onion

dash salt

dash pepper

TIP

⇨ Kalamata olives with a slightly salty dressing make this dish unbeatable. For those of you on a salt-restricted diet, substitute cherry tomatoes for the kalamata olives and use red or yellow bell pepper sliced into wedges across the top.

Greek Cucumber Boats

DRESSING: Combine olive oil, red wine vinegar, dried oregano, red onion, salt and pepper in a covered container. Shake well.

Using a melon baller or teaspoon, scoop out round portions along the length of each cucumber.

Add one pitted kalamata olive in each hole.

Pile red leaf lettuce on top of the olives and then tomatoes.

Finish by drizzling salad dressing along entire length and serve.

(The photo above shows a cucumber with only olives alongside a cucumber fully dressed. This is more to illustrate how to "build" this salad. However, it's actually nice to serve it this way, too.)

CAESAR SALAD

'Be'
Traditional
Recipe

SERVES
2

TIME REQUIRED
35 min
(20 prep + 15 cooking)

Caesar Salad

Preheat oven to 400 degrees.

CROUTONS: Cut the bread into 1 inch squares and put into a large bowl. Add Italian seasoning, salt, olive oil and melted butter and mix well. Line a baking sheet with foil and spread out the seasoned croutons. Bake for 10 minutes, turning midway. Turn off oven but let the croutons sit in the oven for 5 more minutes. Remove and set aside.

CODDLED EGG: To coddle an egg, cook it slightly by placing it (in the shell) into a pot of boiling water. Leave it for about 1 minute. This is long enough to warm the egg inside but not cook it. Remove from the boiling water and set aside.

DRESSING: Prepare the dressing by blending water, lemon juice, Worcestershire, salt, pepper, Parmesan cheese, egg and garlic. Pulse for about 1 minute. On low, slowly add the olive oil to the dressing in your blender a little at a time. Blend for just a minute until it is all incorporated. Set aside.

Take half of a romaine head and lay on your serving plate. Drizzle a heavy portion of dressing and top with croutons and Parmesan cheese. Add salt and pepper to taste.

MAIN DISH

20 slices sourdough bread

1-2 tbsp Italian seasoning

1 tsp salt

3 tbsp olive oil

2 tbsp butter, melted

2 heads of romaine lettuce, halved

Parmesan cheese for garnish

DRESSING

1 egg, coddled

2 tbsp cold water

2 tbsp lemon juice

1 tsp Worcestershire

½ tsp salt

½ tsp black pepper

3 tbsp Parmesan cheese

1 clove pressed garlic

½ cup olive oil

TIP

⇒ Why so many croutons? Make them and you will see why. You'll end up eating half of them before you even serve this dish.

28

'Free'
Allergen-free Recipe

⊘	GLUTEN
⊘	WHEAT
⊘	DAIRY
⊘	CASEIN
⊘	EGG
⊘	NUT
⊘	CORN
⊘	SOY

SERVES
4

TIME REQUIRED
35 min
(20 prep + 15 cooking)

Read all food labels carefully and choose only products that are free of unwanted allergens for use in this recipe.

MAIN DISH

2 cups Rice Chex™ cereal

3 tbsp olive oil

½ tsp fresh rosemary, chopped fine

salt and pepper to taste

2 heads of romaine lettuce, halved

DRESSING

15 oz canned, no salt added, white kidney beans, drained

¼ cup water

1 tbsp white wine vinegar

¼ cup fresh squeezed lemon juice

1 clove garlic, chopped

½ tsp salt

dash of black pepper

3 tbsp olive oil

TIP

⇒ Kidney beans are an excellent way to boost fiber. Even if you're not trying to avoid allergens, this salad dressing is a fantastic one to make frequently.

New Caesar Salad

Preheat the oven to 375 degrees.

CROUTONS: Line a cookie sheet with aluminum foil and spread out Rice Chex™ cereal in a single layer. Add olive oil, chopped rosemary, and salt to taste. Mix gently until all the ingredients come together. Brown in the oven for 3-4 minutes, stirring every minute. Watch closely as the Rice Chex™ can burn easily at this temperature. Once the Chex cereal starts to brown, remove from the oven and let cool.

DRESSING: Prepare your dressing by blending kidney beans, water, vinegar, lemon juice, garlic, salt and black pepper. Pulse for about 1 minute. With blender on low, slowly add the olive oil to the dressing a little at a time, until it is all incorporated. Set aside.

Take half of a romaine head and lay on your serving plate. Drizzle with a heavy portion of dressing and top with croutons. Add salt and pepper to taste.

CITRUS SPINACH SALAD

'Be'
Traditional Recipe

SERVES
2

TIME REQUIRED
20 min
(20 prep + 0 cooking)

MAIN DISH

8 oz fresh spinach

1 small can mandarin oranges, drained

½ grapefruit, segmented

3 tbsp pine nuts

2 oz goat cheese

DRESSING

½ cup light olive oil

¼ cup apple cider vinegar

2 green onions, finely sliced

¼ tsp salt

¼ tsp pepper

2 tsp sugar

1 tsp juice from mandarin orange can

1 tsp grapefruit juice (fresh)

1 tsp lemon juice (fresh)

TIP

⇨ I love how this dressing goes back and forth from sweet to savory in every bite. The soft texture of the cheese with the crunch of the pine nuts will really leave you satisfied.

Citrus Spinach Salad

DRESSING: Add oil, vinegar, onions, salt, pepper, sugar, and fresh squeezed juices into a covered container. Shake well to incorporate.

In a bowl, combine spinach, mandarin oranges and grapefruit. Add the salad dressing and gently toss so all the spinach is covered with dressing.

Divide the salad between two plates.

Top with pine nuts and goat cheese and serve.

'Free'
Allergen-free Recipe

SERVES
2

TIME REQUIRED
10 min
(10 prep + 0 cooking)

⊘ GLUTEN
⊘ WHEAT
⊘ DAIRY
⊘ CASEIN
⊘ EGG
⊘ NUT
⊘ CORN
⊘ SOY

Read all food labels carefully and choose only products that are free of unwanted allergens for use in this recipe.

MAIN DISH

8 oz fresh spinach

6 oz apricots, chopped

½ green apple, peeled and cubed

½ cup salted pepitas (pumpkin seeds)

DRESSING

¼ cup olive oil

3 tbsp apple cider vinegar

¼ tsp salt

¼ tsp pepper

1 tsp apricot jam

2 tbsp lemon juice (fresh)

Apricot Spinach Salad

DRESSING: Add oil, vinegar, salt, pepper, apricot jam and fresh lemon juice into a covered container. Shake well to incorporate.

In a bowl, combine spinach, chopped apricots and apple cubes. Add the salad dressing and gently toss so all the spinach is covered with dressing.

Divide the salad between two plates.

Top with pepitas (pumpkin seeds) and serve.

TIPS

⇨ To keep the apple from browning, toss with a little lemon juice immediately after cutting.

⇨ Personalize this dish by adding your own favorite ingredients, like cranberries or fresh-cut strawberries.

To reduce cross-contamination use cutting boards, towels, utensils, and dish sponges dedicated for allergen-free cooking.

SASSY SUNFLOWER SALAD

'Be'
Traditional Recipe

SERVES
2

TIME REQUIRED
35 min
(20 prep + 15 cooking)

MAIN DISH

2 chicken breasts

2 tbsp fresh lemon juice

2 cloves garlic, pressed

¼ tsp salt

8 oz salad greens

radishes for garnish

DRESSING

3 radishes

1 cloves garlic

3 tbsp olive oil

1 tbsp red wine vinegar

3 tbsp salted sunflower seeds

¼ cup mayonnaise

3 tbsp water

¼ cup packed parsley

¼ cup packed cilantro

1 tsp fresh lemon juice

TIP

⇒ Don't skimp on the radishes!
They add such bold spicy flavor,
making this salad dressing pack
a surprising punch.

Sassy Sunflower Salad

Place chicken breasts in a glass bowl or zip-lock bag. Add lemon juice, pressed garlic and salt for a light marinade. Let the chicken come to room temperature on the counter and sit in the marinade while you make your salad dressing, only 10 to 20 minutes.

DRESSING: In a blender or food processor, add all the salad dressing ingredients. Blend for about 45 seconds with a few short pulses at the beginning (about 5 seconds each), and then a few longer pulses to finish the blending (about 10 seconds each). Blend until becomes smooth.

Get the grill hot to start (about 400°F), lay on the chicken breasts and reduce the heat to low. Cook the chicken 5-7 minutes on each side, keeping the cooking temperature at about 300 degrees. Flip mid-way and only flip once.

Once the chicken is cooked, transfer from the barbecue onto a plate and cover tightly with aluminum foil. This will seal in the juices and steam the chicken slightly.

Assemble the greens on two plates. Slice the chicken breasts into inch-long sections and fan out next to the salad on each plate. Spoon salad dressing over both the salad and chicken and serve immediately.

Garlic Chicken Salad

MARINADE: In a medium sized bowl add parsley, garlic and olive oil and mix well. Add chicken breasts and cover with marinade. Sprinkle with salt and pepper to taste.

DRESSING: In a separate small bowl, add the tomatoes, olive oil, garlic and salt. Mix well.

Get the grill hot to start (about 400 degrees), lay on the chicken breasts and reduce the heat to low. Cook the chicken 5-7 minutes on each side, keeping the cooking temperature at about 300 degrees. Flip mid-way and only flip once.

Once the chicken is cooked, transfer from the barbecue onto a plate and cover tightly with aluminum foil. This will seal in the juices and steam the chicken slightly.

In a large bowl, add the salad greens and the tomato garlic dressing and mix well.

To plate, add half of the dressed salad and one chicken breast. Add 1 tbsp balsamic vinegar (or more to your taste) to the salad greens.

Repeat with the second salad and serve.

GARLIC CHICKEN SALAD

'Free'
Allergen-free Recipe

SERVES

2

TIME REQUIRED

25 min
(10 prep + 15 cooking)

- ⊘ GLUTEN
- ⊘ WHEAT
- ⊘ DAIRY
- ⊘ CASEIN
- ⊘ EGG
- ⊘ NUT
- ⊘ CORN
- ⊘ SOY

Read all food labels carefully and choose only products that are free of unwanted allergens for use in this recipe.

MAIN DISH/MARINADE

¼ cup parsley, chopped

10 cloves garlic, chopped

1½ tbsp olive oil

2 organic chicken breasts

salt and pepper, to taste

8 oz salad greens

DRESSING

½ cup cherry tomatoes, chopped

¼ cup olive oil

1 clove garlic, finely chopped

¼ tsp salt

2-3 tbsp balsamic vinegar

TIP

⇨ This recipe is my sister Julie's favorite. Instead of a single garlic clove in the tomato dressing, she puts in 6! Garlic is packed with potential health benefits, so feel free to add as many cloves as you can stand!

33

To reduce cross-contamination use cutting boards, towels, utensils, and dish sponges dedicated for allergen-free cooking.

FRUITY TOSTADA SALAD

'Be'
Traditional Recipe

SERVES
4

TIME REQUIRED
50 min
(30 prep + 20 cooking)

GLUTEN ⊘
WHEAT ⊘
DAIRY ✓
CASEIN ✓
EGG ⊘
NUT ⊘
CORN ✓
SOY ✓

½ lb ground beef

1 tsp each cumin, onion powder, garlic powder

dash salt and pepper

12 oz shredded lettuce

1 cup tomatoes, diced

15 oz can tropical fruit, drained and chopped

½ cup onion, chopped

¼ cup cilantro

2 tbsp red wine vinegar

8 corn tostada shells

2 avocados, sliced

16 oz can refried beans

1 cup Mexican cheese blend

TIP

⇒ This is a super fun recipe for kids. Put all the ingredients on little plates and they can build their own meal. They can add as much, or as little, of each ingredient as they want. This is a great variation on the traditional make-your-own pizza.

Fruity Tostada Salad

In a sauté pan, brown ground beef over medium heat. Add cumin, onion powder, garlic powder and a dash of salt and pepper. Once cooked through, drain excess fat and set the meat aside.

FRUIT SALSA: Combine diced tomatoes, chopped tropical fruit, onion, cilantro and vinegar. Add dash of salt. Mix well to combine and set aside.

Warm tostada shells in the oven for 5-10 minutes at 350 degrees. Just watch them carefully so they don't burn. Do not microwave them.

While the tostada shells are warming, warm the beans in a small pot on low for 5-10 minutes, stirring frequently. You can also warm the beans in a microwave.

Assemble the tostada by placing a tostada shell on the serving plate and layering with the refried beans, browned ground beef, lettuce, fruit salsa and cheese. Add another tostada and repeat the steps. Top with sliced avocado.

'Free'
Allergen-free
Recipe

SERVES
4

TIME REQUIRED
36 min
(20 prep + 16 cooking)

⊘ GLUTEN
⊘ WHEAT
⊘ DAIRY
⊘ CASEIN
⊘ EGG
⊘ NUT
⊘ CORN
⊘ SOY

Read all food labels carefully and choose only products that are free of unwanted allergens for use in this recipe.

MAIN DISH

8 allergen-free brown rice tortillas

1 tbsp olive oil

1 small red onion, chopped

8 oz grass-fed, organic ground beef

¼ tsp salt

¼ tsp black pepper

1 tsp cumin

1 cup chopped romaine lettuce

1 cup cherry tomatoes, halved

1 avocado, sliced

DRESSING

½ cup cilantro, chopped

3 tbsp red wine vinegar

¼ tsp salt

¼ tsp black pepper

3 tbsp pepitas (pumpkin seeds)

¼ cup olive oil

Savory Tostada Salad

Preheat the oven to 425 degrees.

If the tortillas are larger than 6 inches in diameter (they are often 9 inches in diameter), cut them to be smaller. Toast them in the oven 3 minutes each side, or until they are crisp. Set aside. Reserve the extra pieces for another use. *(I have searched far and wide for store-bought, brown rice tostada shells and just can't find them. A big thanks to my friend Karen for the idea of toasting brown rice tortillas for use in this "Free" Tostada. After trimming the tortillas down to size, I use the leftover pieces to make chips. They're also delicious if you sprinkle them with brown sugar and cinnamon.)*

In a sauté pan over medium heat, add olive oil and red onions and cook for 5 minutes. Add ground beef to the onions, salt and pepper to taste and stir well. Once completely cooked, set aside. Drain the fat if necessary.

DRESSING: In a blender, add cilantro, vinegar, salt, pepper, pepitas and oil. Blend until everything is smooth.

To assemble, place one crisp tortilla shell on a plate. Add 1 tsp of the cilantro dressing and ¼ of the beef and onion mixture. Top with a second crisp tortilla, and ¼ each of the chopped lettuce, tomatoes and avocado. Spoon on one tbsp of the cilantro dressing. Repeat for the remaining servings.

"Free"

GRAINS

✓	GLUTEN
✓	WHEAT
✓	DAIRY
✓	CASEIN
⊘	EGG
⊘	NUT
✓	CORN
✓	SOY

'Be'
Traditional
Recipe

SERVES
4-5

TIME REQUIRED
85 min
(35 prep + 50 cooking)

2 cups chicken stock

1 cup long grain white rice

8 oz sour cream

1 cup onions, chopped

4 oz can diced green chilies

14.5 oz can chopped tomatoes,
   with liquid

1½ cups cheddar cheese, grated

½ cup fresh or frozen corn kernels

1 avocado, sliced

Rice Casserole

Preheat the oven to 400 degrees.

Bring chicken stock to a boil in a large pot, add rice and cover.
Set the timer for 20 minutes. No peeking! The lost steam that is
released when you take the lid off will make the rice dry.

Once the rice is done, add the sour cream, onion, chilies, chopped
tomatoes, and corn. Add 1 cup of the cheddar cheese. Mix well and
spoon into a large casserole dish.

Top with the remaining cheddar cheese and bake for 30 minutes.
If you want a crispy, golden brown cheesy topping, broil for 3-4 minutes.

Let this dish cool for 5-10 minutes before serving. Garnish with avocado.

TIPS

⇒ Easy, easy, easy! This is a super
   meal to make if you are a busy
   person looking for a "throw-it
   together-fast meal". Of course, if
   you have time, sautéing the onions
   and tomatoes in olive oil first
   adds a nice dimension of flavor.

⇒ This dish is a great one to bring
   to a party. It is just cheesy and
   creamy enough to taste awesome,
   but not too heavy.

Mexican Rice

Over medium heat, add olive oil to a medium-size pot that can be covered. Add chopped onion and bell pepper and sauté until tender.

Add the stock, tomato sauce, cumin, cilantro, and salt, and bring to a boil. Add the rice. Reduce heat to low, cover and cook for 20 minutes. No peeking! The lost moisture will make the rice dry.

Once the rice is done, stir well and serve.

MEXICAN RICE

'Free'
Allergen-free Recipe

SERVES
4

TIME REQUIRED
30 min
(5 prep + 25 cooking)

⊘ GLUTEN
⊘ WHEAT
⊘ DAIRY
⊘ CASEIN
⊘ EGG
⊘ NUT
⊘ CORN
⊘ SOY

Read all food labels carefully and choose only products that are free of unwanted allergens for use in this recipe.

2 tbsp olive oil

½ small yellow onion, chopped

½ bell pepper, chopped

2 cups organic, allergen-free chicken stock

8 oz can tomato sauce

½ tsp cumin

1 tbsp cilantro, chopped

½ tsp sea salt

1 cup long grain rice

TIPS

⇒ Yet another recipe where you basically throw it all in a pan, quickly sauté and come back 20 minutes later. It makes the house smell so good and the end result is a mouth-watering crowd pleaser.

⇒ Mexican rice is served in so many ways that you can almost add anything and still call it Mexican rice. Try adding diced green chilies, garlic, parsley, or other seasonings to make it your own.

39

To reduce cross-contamination use cutting boards, towels, utensils, and dish sponges dedicated for allergen-free cooking.

PARMESAN COUSCOUS CUPS

'Be'
Traditional Recipe

SERVES
6

TIME REQUIRED
50 min
(20 prep + 20-30 cooking)

6 oz shredded Parmesan cheese

6 tbsp butter, divided into thirds

1 tbsp olive oil

1 garlic clove, chopped

4 green onions, chopped

1 cup water

1 cup couscous

5 oz sliced crimini mushrooms

½ tsp red pepper flakes

TIPS

⇒ Use a baking stone to bake your Parmesan cheese if you have one. A parchment paper lined cookie sheet works, too.

⇒ The Parmesan cups get easier to make after you get used to it. Eating the ones that don't quite turn out perfect is the best part!

Parmesan Couscous Cups

Preheat the oven to 375 degrees.

PARMESAN CUPS: Spread one ounce of Parmesan cheese into a solid circle on a baking sheet. Bake for 10 minutes so it melts into a disk. Let the cheese rest for 5 minutes before removing. It needs to be cool enough to transfer without tearing, but slightly warm so you can shape it. Use an upside down, small drinking glass or shot glass (about 2½" diameter) and rest your cheese disk on top. Push it down around the sides to form a cup. Repeat 5 more times. Let the cheese cups completely cool before turning over and filling.

COUSCOUS: Melt 2 tbsp butter and olive oil over medium heat in a medium sized pot. Add garlic and 2 chopped green onions. Sauté for a few minutes. Sprinkle with salt. Add the couscous and mix everything together for about 2 minutes. Add 1 cup of water to the pot, stir, and remove from heat and cover for 5 minutes. While the couscous is resting, add 2 tbsp butter to a sauté pan and melt over medium heat. Add the remaining 2 chopped green onions. Sauté for about 2 minutes.

Add the crimini mushrooms. Sauté for only a few minutes. Don't over cook them. Once they get slightly soft and release a little moisture, take off the heat. Sprinkle with a little salt and red pepper flakes.

Go back to the couscous which now is light and fluffy. Bring the pot back to the stove over medium heat, add the remaining 2 tbsp butter. Stir well. Now put it all together! Grab a Parmesan cup, fill with couscous and top with your crimini mushrooms.
Serve immediately.

BALSAMIC PORTOBELLO QUINOA

⊘	GLUTEN
⊘	WHEAT
⊘	DAIRY
⊘	CASEIN
⊘	EGG
⊘	NUT
⊘	CORN
⊘	SOY

'Free'
Allergen-free
Recipe

SERVES
4

TIME REQUIRED
50 min
(15 prep + 35 cooking)

Read all food labels carefully and choose only products that are free of unwanted allergens for use in this recipe.

1 cup parsley, chopped

4 heads garlic, chopped

½ cup + 2 tbsp olive oil, divided:
    ½ cup for marinade
    2 tbsp for sauté

4 portobello mushrooms,
    stems removed

2 shallots, chopped

salt & pepper to taste

1¼ cup organic, allergen-free
    chicken or vegetable stock

1 cup quinoa

¾ cup balsamic vinegar

1 tsp organic sugar

1 red bell pepper, quartered

Balsamic Portobello Quinoa

Combine chopped parsley, garlic, and ½ cup olive oil in a large plastic bag. Add the 4 mushroom caps and bell peppers and gently work the mixture around the vegetables. Seal and let stand at room temperature while you prepare the rest of the dish.

In a medium pot, add 2 tbsp olive oil over medium heat. Add shallots and sauté until limp, about 5 minutes. Season with salt and pepper. Add broth and bring to a boil. Add quinoa and reduce heat to low. Cook according to package instructions.

BALSAMIC GLAZE: To prepare the balsamic glaze, bring ¾ cup balsamic vinegar to a boil. Add sugar and stir, over medium high heat, until the vinegar reduces by half. Stir frequently. This will become thick and look like syrup. Remove from heat and set aside.

Barbecue bell peppers and mushroom over medium heat on the grill. Start the mushrooms gill side down. After about 5 minutes, flip all the vegetables and reduce heat to low. Fill the mushroom cups with the parsley and garlic mixture. Sprinkle salt and pepper on all the vegetables. Cook for 5 more minutes.

Cut the bell peppers into thin strips. Lay strips of bell pepper on top of each mushroom.

To plate, add one scoop quinoa and top with one mushroom. Drizzle balsamic glaze over the dish and serve immediately.

TIP

⇒ If you don't have (or don't like) quinoa, cooked rice works great, too.

LASAGNA QUINOA

'Be'
Traditional Recipe

SERVES
6

TIME REQUIRED
70 min
(20 prep + 50 cooking)

1 cup quinoa

2½ cups chicken stock, divided
    2 cups for cooking quinoa
    ½ cup for red pepper sauce

3 tbsp olive oil

2 red bell peppers, chopped

1 small yellow onion, chopped

2 cloves garlic, chopped

½ tsp salt

1 cup cheddar cheese, shredded

1 cup mozzarella cheese, shredded

TIPS

⇒ When I sat down to dream up a creative and tasty recipe that included quinoa, I tapped into my Italian ancestry for inspiration. This is my version of lasagna, but quinoa-style. The texture and taste of this dish will amaze you!

⇒ Wondering why there are gluten, corn and soy in this dish? Blame it on the chicken stock. Read labels carefully and choose an allergen-free stock if you want to avoid those ingredients.

Lasagna Quinoa

Preheat the oven to 400 degrees.

In a medium pot, bring 2 cups of stock to a boil. Add quinoa, stir well, cover, and turn heat to low. Cook for 20 minutes or until liquid is gone. Take off heat once done and set aside.

RED PEPPER SAUCE: Add olive oil to a large sauté pan over medium-high heat. Add bell peppers, onions, garlic, and salt, and sauté for 5 minutes. If the heat is too low, the vegetables will not brown. You want them to develop a little color, but be careful not to burn them. Once the vegetables are sautéed, place them in a blender or food processor, along with ½ cup chicken stock and blend to make the sauce.

Pour half of the red pepper sauce into an 8 x 8 baking dish. Spoon half of the cooked quinoa over the layer of sauce. Top with ½ cup mozzarella and ½ cup cheddar cheese.

Repeat with ¼ cup sauce, the remaining quinoa, ½ cup mozzarella, and ½ cup cheddar cheese.

Top with remaining sauce and bake for 30 minutes.

'Free'
Allergen-free
Recipe

⊘	GLUTEN
⊘	WHEAT
⊘	DAIRY
⊘	CASEIN
⊘	EGG
⊘	NUT
⊘	CORN
⊘	SOY

SERVES
4

TIME REQUIRED
35 min
(15 prep + 20 cooking)

Read all food labels carefully and choose only products that are free of unwanted allergens for use in this recipe.

MAIN DISH

2 cups water

1 cup quinoa

2 green onions, chopped

¼ cup mint, chopped

½ cup parsley, chopped

½ cup cucumber, peeled and diced

½ cup cherry tomatoes, halved

DRESSING

¼ cup olive oil

¼ cup fresh lemon juice

¼ tsp salt

¼ tsp black pepper

TIP

⇨ Not all lemons are the same: some lemons are very sweet while others are tart. If you find your dressing is too tart, just add a pinch of sugar.

Tabbouleh Quinoa

In a medium pot, bring water to a boil. Add quinoa, stir well, cover, and turn heat to low. Cook for 20 minutes or until liquid is gone.

To the quinoa, add the green onions, mint, parsley, cucumber, and cherry tomatoes. Mix well.

(This dish is a favorite of mine to make during summer because the lemon and mint make it so light and refreshing. Feel free to add more of the vegetables and greens to your taste. If you want added flavor, consider adding cubed avocado or a sprinkle of cayenne pepper.)

DRESSING: In a small sealable container, add the dressing ingredients: olive oil, lemon juice, salt, and pepper. Shake well to incorporate.

Drizzle the dressing over the quinoa and mix again. Serve warm or cold for a delicious meal.

MOZZARELLA BARLEY CAKES

'Be'
Traditional
Recipe

SERVES
6-8

TIME REQUIRED
70 min
(10 prep + 45-60 cooking)

1 cup pearl barley

3 green onions, chopped

½ red bell pepper, chopped

½ Anaheim chili, chopped

½ cup + 2 tbsp olive oil

¼ tsp salt

1 cup Parmesan cheese

1½ cups mozzarella cheese

2 eggs

1 cup bread crumbs

TIPS

⇒ These cooked barley cakes taste so good both hot and cold. They make a tasty and filling breakfast!

⇒ It's tricky to get them to stick together and fry up perfectly at first. Once you get the hang of it, you will be cooking these all the time.

Mozzarella Barley Cakes

Cook the barley according to package instructions.

While barley is cooking, sauté onions, bell peppers, and chili in 2 tbsp olive oil for about 5 minutes over medium heat. Add salt and brown slightly, but do not burn. Set aside.

Once the barley is cooked, put it into a large mixing bowl. Add the sautéed vegetables, Parmesan cheese and mozzarella cheese to the barley. Combine well.

Break eggs into a bowl and whisk well. Add eggs to the barley mixture and mix well.

Pour bread crumbs on a plate. Working like an assembly line, use an ice cream scoop (or spoon) to scoop up some of the barley mixture, and roll it in a ball in the palm of your hands. Then press down to make it into a flat cake. Cover each side completely with bread crumbs and lay on a cookie sheet. Repeat until all of the mixture is gone.

Add about ¼ cup oil to a large sauté pan and fry up each cake over medium heat for about 3 minutes each side. If the crumbs in the oil start to burn, start over with new oil. Don't overcrowd the pan. Cook two at a time so flipping is easy and the temperature stays even. If they are frying too quickly, turn the heat down to medium low and cook until golden brown.

SAVORY RICE CAKES

‘Free’
Allergen-free
Recipe

SERVES
6-8

TIME REQUIRED
55 min
(10 prep + 45 cooking)

⊘	GLUTEN
⊘	WHEAT
⊘	DAIRY
⊘	CASEIN
⊘	EGG
⊘	NUT
⊘	CORN
⊘	SOY

Read all food labels carefully and choose only products that are free of unwanted allergens for use in this recipe.

1 cup coconut milk

1 cup organic, allergen-free chicken stock

1 cup basmati rice

½ tsp cumin

½ tsp garlic powder

¼ tsp tumeric

¼ tsp salt

1 jalapeño pepper or Anaheim chili

2 green onions

½ cup allergen-free bread crumbs

TIPS

⇨ You can skip the breading and baking and serve just the Thai-flavored rice. Either way, it's hearty and delicious!

⇨ If you can't find bread crumbs that are completely allergen-free, use Rice Chex™ cereal and crush them in a blender.

Savory Rice Cakes

In a pot, bring the coconut milk and chicken stock to a boil.

Add basmati rice, cumin, garlic powder, turmeric, salt, and jalapeño or Anaheim chili and stir well.

Reduce heat to low, cover, and cook 40 minutes. No peeking.

Once the rice is cooked, stir well to incorporate all of the ingredients. Let this cool for several minutes so it's not too hot to handle.

Once the rice is cool enough to touch, add the green onions and mix well. Form the rice mixture into 6-8 patties.

Put bread crumbs on a large plate. Cover each rice patty, on both sides, with the crumbs. Press the crumbs into the cakes so they stay in place.

Put the cakes in a baking dish and broil on high, uncovered, for just a few minutes, until golden brown.

Checklist

✓	GLUTEN
✓	WHEAT
✓	DAIRY
✓	CASEIN
⊘	EGG
⊘	NUT
✓	CORN
✓	SOY

PROSCIUTTO PILAF

'Be'
Traditional Recipe

SERVES
4

TIME REQUIRED
65 min
(10 prep + 55 cooking)

1 head garlic

2 tbsp olive oil

2 tbsp butter

1 cup white onion, chopped

1 cup peas, fresh or frozen

1 cup long grain rice

2 cups chicken stock

2-3 oz prosciutto, chopped

3 saffron threads

½ cup Parmesan cheese, shaved

¼ cup parsley, garnish

TIPS

⇨ Roasting garlic is well worth the time it takes. To make that time even more useful, roast 3 or 4 heads of garlic and refrigerate them for later use in almost any savory dish. But of course, the busy chef can always just use 2-3 cloves chopped garlic, too!

⇨ Saffron is expen$ive! Luckily, a little goes a long way. But if you need to economize, use 1/2 tsp turmeric for color instead of saffron.

Prosciutto Pilaf

Preheat the oven to 400 degrees.

Cut the top off of 1 head of garlic. Drizzle with olive oil, place in a cupcake tray, cover with foil, and bake for 35 minutes.

In a medium pot, add 2 tbsp butter and 1 tbsp olive oil over medium heat. Once the butter melts, add the onions and peas and sauté for 2-3 minutes.

Add the rice and stir for 2 more minutes.

Add chicken broth, prosciutto, and saffron threads. Stir well and bring to a boil. Once it comes to a boil, reduce heat to low, cover and cook for 20 minutes. No peeking!

Once the rice is cooked, fluff a bit with a fork. Add Parmesan cheese and stir well. Add parsley and extra Parmesan cheese to garnish.

46

'Free'
Allergen-free Recipe

SERVES
4-6

TIME REQUIRED
70 min
(10 prep + 60 cooking)

⊘ GLUTEN
⊘ WHEAT
⊘ DAIRY
⊘ CASEIN
⊘ EGG
⊘ NUT
⊘ CORN
⊘ SOY

Read all food labels carefully and choose only products that are free of unwanted allergens for use in this recipe.

4 tbsp olive oil

½ red bell pepper, chopped

½ medium onion, chopped

1 small jalapeño, chopped

2 garlic cloves, chopped

3 cups organic, allergen-free vegetable stock

1 cup jasmine or brown rice

½ cup wild rice

½ tsp salt

Multigrain Pilaf

Add olive oil to a stock pot over medium heat and sauté the red bell pepper for 5 minutes. Add onion, jalapeno, and garlic and continue to sauté for several more minutes until the onions and peppers become soft.

Add stock and bring to a boil. Add jasmine or brown rice and wild rice, reduce heat to low, and cook for 50 minutes. No peeking! If after the 50 minutes it looks like there is still liquid remaining, cook for another 5 minutes uncovered, or until all of the liquid evaporates.

Once completely cooked, add the salt, mix well, and serve.

TIP

⇒ The heavy olive oil here adds a lot of flavor, so don't skimp on it. If you're worried about the calories, all you need to do is add a little more activity to your day. Take the stairs instead of the elevator, play ball with your kids outside, or go for a quick walk at some point in the day. A little activity in your day means extra flavor in your food!

✓	GLUTEN
✓	WHEAT
✓	DAIRY
✓	CASEIN
⊘	EGG
⊘	NUT
✓	CORN
⊘	SOY

HOME-STYLE BISCUITS

'Be'
Traditional Recipe

SERVES
10 biscuits

TIME REQUIRED
25 min
(10 prep + 15 cooking)

2 cups unbleached all-purpose flour

1 stick butter, chopped into small cubes,
    plus 2 tbsp butter, melted

1 tsp salt

1 tbsp baking powder

½ tbsp baking soda

½ cup + 2 tbsp milk

½ tsp vanilla

TIPS

⇨ I know you're thinking, "That's a TON of butter!" And you're right. This is why these biscuits are so flaky and delicious. The key is to eat these in moderation and pair it with a little exercise, so you have a delicious treat and no guilt. Go ahead and indulge— it's so worth it. Now get on that treadmill!

⇨ These biscuits freeze well for a quick addition to any meal.

Home-style Biscuits

Preheat the oven to 425 degrees.

In a large mixing bowl, combine flour, cubed butter, salt, baking powder, and baking soda. Mix well.

In a separate bowl, add the milk and vanilla. Whisk to combine.

Add the liquid ingredients, a little at a time, into the flour mixture and work into a dough. If the dough is too crumbly, add one tsp of milk at a time until it comes together. Place the dough on a floured cutting board and spread it out, with either your hands or a rolling pin, to a thickness of about ½ inch.

With a 2-3 inch diameter cookie cutter or a drinking glass, stamp out the biscuits.

Bake on a baking stone or cookie sheet for 10-15 minutes or until golden brown.

Once the biscuits have finished baking, brush melted butter on top just prior to serving.

48

'Free'
Allergen-free
Recipe

⊘	GLUTEN
⊘	WHEAT
⊘	DAIRY
⊘	CASEIN
⊘	EGG
⊘	NUT
⊘	CORN
⊘	SOY

SERVES
12
biscuits

TIME REQUIRED
20 min
(10 prep + 10 cooking)

Read all food labels carefully and choose only products that are free of unwanted allergens for use in this recipe.

¾ cup potato starch

1½ cup rice flour

1 tbsp baking soda

¼ tsp salt

2 tbsp fine granulated sugar

¾ cup rice milk

¼ cup rice-bran oil

1 tsp vanilla

Rice Biscuits

Preheat the oven to 400 degrees.

Combine potato starch, rice flour, baking soda, salt, and sugar in a large mixing bowl. Stir well.

In a separate bowl, combine rice milk, oil, and vanilla. Whisk together.

Slowly add the liquid to the dry ingredients, and mix with a spoon until it gets thick.

Spread the mixture, which should be a little crumbly, onto a cutting board lined with parchment paper. Knead the dough out into an even circle that is about 1 inch thick.

With a 2-3 inch diameter cookie cutter or a drinking glass, stamp out the biscuits.

Line an allergen-free baking stone or cookie sheet with parchment paper. Cook for 8-10 minutes until golden brown.

TIP

⇒ These biscuits are great paired with your favorite jam or preserves. I like to stack these biscuits 3 layers high with fresh strawberries and blueberries in between. Top with a sprig of mint and you have the most delicious and allergen-free dessert in town!

✓	GLUTEN
✓	WHEAT
⊘	DAIRY
⊘	CASEIN
⊘	EGG
⊘	NUT
✓	CORN
✓	SOY

'Be'
Traditional
Recipe

SERVES
20
squares

TIME REQUIRED
30 min
(10 prep + 20 cooking)

2 tbsp olive oil

1 tsp fresh rosemary, chopped

2-3 cloves garlic, pressed

½ tsp red pepper flakes

½ tsp salt

3 cups chicken stock

1 cup fine ground corn meal

5-7 long rosemary stems
   to use as skewers

TIPS

⇒ These polenta squares are delicious. I love them right out of the refrigerator, grilled on the BBQ, or even warm from the oven.

⇒ If you want to make this more of a meal instead of a side dish, use 4 parts cooking liquid to one part fine corn meal. Top with sautéed mushrooms and serve right away while it's hot and creamy. Serve alongside a salad, or with a grilled lamb chop, and you have one tasty, inexpensive, and filling meal.

Rosemary Squares

Warm olive oil in a pot over medium heat. Add chopped rosemary, garlic, and red pepper flakes and cook for a few minutes. Add salt and stir well.

Add the chicken stock and bring to a boil. Add corn meal, reduce heat to low, and whisk well to avoid lumps.

The corn meal will thicken over time. Switch to a spoon midway and continue stirring every few minutes to keep the corn meal, now polenta, smooth.

Once the polenta is cooked through, pour into a lightly greased 8"x 8"x 2" pan and let cool completely before cutting. You can refrigerate for faster cooling.

Once cool, cut into squares and skewer with rosemary stems. Wooden or metal skewers work great, too.

'Free'
Allergen-free Recipe

SERVES
20 squares

TIME REQUIRED
50 min
(10 prep + 40 cooking)

⊘	GLUTEN
⊘	WHEAT
⊘	DAIRY
⊘	CASEIN
⊘	EGG
⊘	NUT
⊘	CORN
⊘	SOY

Read all food labels carefully and choose only products that are free of unwanted allergens for use in this recipe.

1¾ cups organic, allergen-free chicken stock, divided

½ cup quinoa grain

2 large russet potatoes, peeled and cubed

1 tbsp + 1 tsp, olive oil

2 green onions, chopped

1 Anaheim chili, chopped

½ tsp fresh rosemary, chopped

1 tsp salt

Quinoa Potato Squares

Preheat the oven to 400 degrees.

Add 1 cup of chicken stock to a pot. Bring to a boil, add the quinoa grain, and reduce heat to low. Cook covered and according to package directions, usually about 25 minutes.

Bring a medium-sized pot of water to a boil. Add cubed potatoes and cook until the potatoes are completely soft. Drain the potatoes in a colander and place back into the pot. Add ¾ cup chicken stock and mash well, until a smooth consistency. Add more chicken stock (or water) 1 tbsp at a time, if needed.

In a sauté pan, add 1 tbsp of olive oil over medium heat. Add green onions, Anaheim chili, and rosemary and cook until completely soft and slightly brown.

To the mashed potatoes, add the cooked quinoa and sautéed onions, chili, and rosemary. Add 1 tsp salt and mix well.

Add 1 tsp olive oil to an 8" x 8" baking dish. Spread oil over inside of dish to help prevent the mixture from sticking. Fold in the potatoes and quinoa mixture. Bake for 10 minutes.

When baking is finished, use a knife to cut 20 squares. Use a fork to gently remove each square from the dish. They are not firm, so be careful. Assemble on a tray and serve.

TIPS

⇒ Mashed potatoes just got better! By adding quinoa, you get a little crunch in your mouth along with a whole lot of protein, too.

⇒ Of course, you could just serve this tasty creation in a bowl, similar to traditional mashed potatoes. But serving these delicious quinoa squares along with chicken or salad makes for a unique presentation.

51

To reduce cross-contamination use cutting boards, towels, utensils, and dish sponges dedicated for allergen-free cooking.

✓	GLUTEN
✓	WHEAT
⊘	DAIRY
⊘	CASEIN
⊘	EGG
⊘	NUT
✓	CORN
✓	SOY

'Be'
Traditional
Recipe

SERVES
4 slices

TIME REQUIRED
25 min
(10 prep + 15 cooking)

3-4 slices French or sourdough
    baguette bread

1 whole garlic clove, for the bread

1-2 garlic cloves, chopped

1 cup seeded Roma tomatoes,
    chopped

2 tsp olive oil

pinch salt

5 basil leaves, chopped

Tomato Basil Bruschetta

Preheat the oven to 375 degrees.

Toast slices of bread for 5 minutes. Remove from oven and set aside.

Rub the garlic clove back and forth on the toasted bread to transfer the garlic oil onto the bread.

In a medium sauté pan, cook garlic and tomatoes in olive oil over medium heat for about 5-10 minutes. Add a pinch of salt.

Add the chopped basil and cook 2 more minutes.

Lay the toasted bread slices out on a platter. Spoon the tomato mixture onto the bread and enjoy.

TIPS

⇒ Simple and delicious. These two words really capture the essence of this dish. So flavorful, yet so easy to prepare.

⇒ This is one of my favorite appetizers for a party. It's easy to double or triple the recipe to make as many as you need. But good luck getting them to your party. I usually eat half while I am making them. So plan ahead and make extra. Trust me!

52

'Free'
Allergen-free
Recipe

SERVES
1 cup of
sauce

TIME REQUIRED
40 min
(10 prep + 30 cooking)

⊘ GLUTEN
⊘ WHEAT
⊘ DAIRY
⊘ CASEIN
⊘ EGG
⊘ NUT
⊘ CORN
⊘ SOY

*Read all food labels carefully and choose
only products that are free of unwanted
allergens for use in this recipe.*

1 to 1½ lbs eggplant
   (about 3/4 cup roasted)

1 tsp olive oil

8 oz jar oil-packed, allergen-free
   sundried tomatoes

1 clove garlic, chopped

1 tsp salt

½ cup basil leaves, chopped

allergen-free bread or crackers

Eggplant Bruschetta

Preheat the oven to 350 degrees.

Cut the stem off of the eggplant, and remove the skin. Slice the eggplant in
half. Spread 1 tsp olive oil on a foil lined cookie sheet and place the eggplant
cut side down. Roast for 30 minutes, or until completely soft.

Let the eggplant cool for several minutes. Chop into small pieces.

Add the chopped eggplant, sundried tomatoes (including oil), garlic, salt,
and basil into a food processor. Blend for a soft, smooth consistency. If it's too
thick, you can add a tablespoon of water, or even olive oil.

Put a spoonful on each cracker or bread slice and serve. You could also fill a
bowl with the bruschetta mixture with the crackers, bread, or even vegetable
sticks alongside.

TIPS

⇒ This dish is so delicious! It makes
for a perfect party appetizer or
as a great pasta sauce. It's so
versatile, there's no limit to the
number of ways you can enjoy it.

⇒ If you don't have a food processor,
you can chop the mixture well by
hand for a chunky, but equally
delicious version of this recipe.

"Free"

PASTA

MACARONI 'N
CHEESE

✓	GLUTEN
✓	WHEAT
✓	DAIRY
✓	CASEIN
⃠	EGG
⃠	NUT
✓	CORN
✓	SOY

'Be'
Traditional
Recipe

SERVES
4-6

TIME REQUIRED
57 min
(15 prep + 42 cooking)

8 oz shell pasta

2 cups heavy cream

several dashes white pepper

1 tsp dry ground mustard

¼ tsp salt

1 cup shredded fontina

1 cup shredded cheddar

1 cup shredded jack

1 cup grated Parmesan cheese

½ cup bread crumbs, panko style

TIPS

⇨ Don't be afraid of the calories in this dish. As I have said before, you need food to fuel your body. Eat a moderate portion and then go out and use that energy to enjoy life.

⇨ Use any combination of your favorite cheeses in this dish. It's so delicious. Yum yum!

Macaroni 'n Cheese

Preheat the oven to 350 degrees.

Bring a large pot of water to a boil. Add the pasta and cook for a few minutes less than package instructions. This will allow for further baking time in the oven.

Add heavy cream to a large sauté pan and simmer over medium high heat. Add white pepper, dry mustard, and salt. Add in one cup of cheese at a time and stir well until all the cheese has melted.

After the pasta is finished cooking, drain well, and add to a casserole dish.

Pour the cheese sauce over the cooked shell pasta. Stir well to incorporate.

Top with panko bread crumbs and bake in the oven for 30 minutes or until golden brown.

GLUTEN

WHEAT

DAIRY

CASEIN

EGG

NUT

CORN

SOY

'Free'
Allergen-free Recipe

SERVES
4

TIME REQUIRED
45 min
(10 prep + 35 cooking)

Read all food labels carefully and choose only products that are free of unwanted allergens for use in this recipe.

8 oz allergen-free shell pasta

3 tbsp olive oil

½ cup yellow onion, chopped

½ cup frozen peas

½ cup cherry tomatoes, quartered

¾ cup organic, allergen-free chicken stock

1½ cups rice milk

4 thin slices allergen-free cooked ham, chopped

½ cup crushed potato chips, low sodium

salt, black pepper, chili flakes, optional

Macaroni 'n Peas

Preheat the oven to 350 degrees.

Bring a large pot of water to a boil. Add the pasta and cook for a few minutes less than package instructions. This will allow for further baking time in the oven.

In a separate pot, add the olive oil over medium heat and sauté the onions until they become translucent. Add in the peas and cherry tomatoes and cook for 5 more minutes, or until the peas have completely defrosted.

Add to this mixture the chicken broth and rice milk and simmer over medium heat. Add in the chopped ham.

Once the pasta is done, drain it well and separate the pasta among 4 medium sized ramekins. Alternatively, you could also bake in a single baking dish.

Pour the broth and rice milk mixture among the 4 cups. Add salt, black pepper, and chili flakes if you'd like it a little spicier, and then mix each ramekin well. Top each ramekin with crushed potato chips.

Bake for 20 minutes, or until it is bubbly and slightly golden brown.

TIPS

⇒ This also makes for an awesome soup. Increase the liquid to 2 cups rice milk and 1 cup chicken stock, and skip the chips and baking.

⇒ Gluten-free pasta may contain corn meal, so consider using brown rice pasta if you're looking to avoid corn.

57

✓	GLUTEN
✓	WHEAT
✓	DAIRY
✓	CASEIN
⊘	EGG
⊘	NUT
⊘	CORN
⊘	SOY

PROSCIUTTO PASTA

'Be'
Traditional Recipe

SERVES
3-4

TIME REQUIRED
25 min
(10 prep + 15 cooking)

8 oz penne pasta

2 tbsp olive oil

½ cup frozen or fresh peas

2 cloves garlic, sliced

3 oz sliced prosciutto,
 cut into small pieces

8 oz mascarpone cheese

8 oz tomato sauce

pinch cayenne pepper or
 red pepper flakes

TIPS

⇒ Mascarpone cheese is like a magic potion in this dish. Your mouth will explode when you taste all that the cheese, peas, and proscuitto have to offer. Even people who don't like the taste of cream sauces will love this dish.

⇒ This is my favorite dish to serve when I have my Italian friends and family over. A stunner of a meal with classic Italian ingredients! Molto bene!

Prosciutto Pasta

Bring a large pot of water to a boil and cook pasta according to instructions.

In a large sauté pan, heat the olive oil over medium heat. Add peas and garlic and sauté for a few minutes. Watch carefully so the garlic doesn't burn.

Add the prosciutto and stir well. Add mascarpone cheese and stir well. Add tomato sauce and continue to stir. Make sure the heat is medium low so it doesn't boil but stays warm.

Add red pepper flakes or cayenne pepper to the sauce.

Once the pasta is done, drain well. Add all of the pasta into the sauté pan with the sauce. Gently mix the pasta until all of it is coated.

Plate, serve, and enjoy.

'Free'
Allergen-free Recipe

SERVES
3-4

TIME REQUIRED
30 min
(10 prep + 20 cooking)

⊘ GLUTEN
⊘ WHEAT
⊘ DAIRY
⊘ CASEIN
⊘ EGG
⊘ NUT
⊘ CORN
⊘ SOY

Read all food labels carefully and choose only products that are free of unwanted allergens for use in this recipe.

8 oz allergen-free penne pasta

1 lb mild or hot allergen-free Italian sausage

3 tbsp olive oil

½ red onion, chopped

4 cloves garlic, chopped

½ cup organic, allergen-free chicken or beef stock

½ cup Italian parsley, chopped

salt and pepper to taste

TIPS

⇒ The sausage in this dish brings such bold flavor and texture. Other great additions to this recipe would be mushrooms, peas, olives, or even artichoke hearts. Whatever your favorite meats and veggies are, try them out with this basic sauce as the foundation.

⇒ If you don't like parsley, use basil or spinach. I love that this has a light sauce; but if you prefer more sauce, simply double the amount of wine, remembering to give it time to reduce.

Sausage Pasta

Bring a large pot of water to a boil and cook pasta according to instructions.

Take the casing off of the sausage. Put the sausage in a large non-stick sauté pan and cook over medium heat until the sausage is fully cooked. Put the cooked sausage in a strainer to drain the fat.

In the same sauté pan you used to cook the sausage, add olive oil over medium heat. Add onions and garlic and sauté until tender. Add the stock and chopped parsley. Simmer for about 5 minutes and reduce the liquid by half.

Add the cooked sausage and mix well.

Once the pasta has finished cooking, drain it well and place into a large serving bowl. Add the sauce to the pasta, mix well, and serve.

(White wine is a fantastic substitute for stock. Just check with your dining companions to see if wine causes a reaction before using.)

✓	GLUTEN
✓	WHEAT
⊘	DAIRY
⊘	CASEIN
✓	EGG
⊘	NUT
⊘	CORN
✓	SOY

'Be'
Traditional
Recipe

SERVES
2-3

TIME REQUIRED
17 min
(5 prep + 12 cooking)

8 oz macaroni pasta

4-5 tbsp mayonnaise

1 tbsp yellow onion, chopped

¾ cup celery, chopped

2 oz can sliced black olives, drained

¼ tsp salt

pepper to taste

TIPS

⇒ This is the way fast food should be... fresh, fast, easy, and delicious.

⇒ I love this pasta hot or cold. It keeps well in the refrigerator, too, so you can make this a day ahead to save on time.

⇒ Add more or less of any of the ingredients to suit your taste. I love extra celery in this dish and when I want things spicy, I double the chopped raw onion. Add more mayonnaise if you like creamier pasta salad. Marinated artichoke hearts are a delicious and filling addition to this recipe, too.

Picnic Pasta

Bring a large pot of water to a boil and cook pasta according to instructions.

Drain the pasta well and place in a serving bowl.

Add mayonnaise, onion, celery, and black olives and mix well.

Add salt and pepper and serve.

'Free'
Allergen-free
Recipe

SERVES
2-3

TIME REQUIRED
25 min
(10 prep + 15 cooking)

⊘	GLUTEN
⊘	WHEAT
⊘	DAIRY
⊘	CASEIN
⊘	EGG
⊘	NUT
⊘	CORN
⊘	SOY

Read all food labels carefully and choose only products that are free of unwanted allergens for use in this recipe.

MAIN DISH

8 oz allergen-free macaroni pasta

1 cup cherry tomatoes, halved

¼ cup basil, chopped

2 oz allergen-free sliced salami, cut into strips

DRESSING

5 tbsp olive oil

2 tbsp lemon juice

1 tbsp red wine vinegar

½ tsp allergen-free Italian seasoning

½ tsp salt

pepper to taste

Italian Pasta

Bring a large pot of water to a boil and cook pasta according to instructions.

DRESSING: While the pasta is cooking, prepare the dressing. In a container with a lid, mix together the olive oil, lemon juice, vinegar, Italian seasoning, salt, and pepper. Shake well to combine.

Once the pasta is done cooking, drain well and place in a serving bowl.

Add the tomatoes, basil, and salami to the pasta and mix well. Add the dressing and mix again.

Serve warm or cold.

TIP

⇒ You will just love the freshness of ripe tomatoes and basil and the zest of the salami and lemon in the dressing. It's a great dish on a hot summer day and travels well for a nice picnic.

✓	GLUTEN
✓	WHEAT
⊘	DAIRY
⊘	CASEIN
✓	EGG
⊘	NUT
✓	CORN
✓	SOY

'Be'
Traditional
Recipe

SERVES
4

TIME REQUIRED
25 min
(5 prep + 20 cooking)

2 tbsp olive oil

1 cup onion, chopped

1 cup tomatoes, chopped

1 small jalapeño, seeded and
    chopped

2 cloves garlic, chopped

12 oz fideo or vermicelli pasta

14 oz chicken stock

2 cups water

¼ cup cilantro

TIPS

⇨ This dish is a light yet bold meal
   for everyone. The flavor of the
   chicken broth and the surprisingly
   gentle spice from the jalapeño
   make this a crowd-pleasing
   dish. Top with cotija cheese and
   avocados to make it even more
   dramatic.

⇨ If you have never heard of or
   cooked with fideo before, give
   it a try. It's always fun to try
   something new. If you can't find
   fideo in your local market, a great
   substitution would be angel hair
   pasta.

Jalapeño Pasta

In a large sauté pan heat olive oil over medium heat.

Sauté onions, tomatoes, jalapeños and garlic for about 5 minutes.

Break up the coils of fideo a bit. Add them into the sauté pan and stir well.

Add chicken stock and water. Make sure the fideo is totally submerged.

Cook over medium heat until the liquid evaporates, about 10-15 minutes, and the fideo is cooked completely.

Serve garnished with cilantro.

'Free'
Allergen-free
Recipe

SERVES
2-3

TIME REQUIRED
25 min
(5 prep + 20 cooking)

⊘ GLUTEN
⊘ WHEAT
⊘ DAIRY
⊘ CASEIN
⊘ EGG
⊘ NUT
⊘ CORN
⊘ SOY

Read all food labels carefully and choose only products that are free of unwanted allergens for use in this recipe.

8 oz allergen-free spaghetti or vermicelli pasta

8 oz can tomato sauce

4 oz allergen-free salsa, fresh or bottled

¼ tsp cumin

Salsa Pasta

Break up the long pasta strands.

In a large sauté pan, add pasta, tomato sauce, salsa, cumin, and enough water to cover the pasta.

Bring to a boil, reduce to simmer, and cook the pasta according to package instructions.

If there is more liquid than you like, cook uncovered on medium until it has evaporated. Conversely, add more liquid at the end if you want a thinner version.

TIPS

⇨ Easy just got easier! It's almost hard to believe you can cook a pasta dish with a homemade sauce in the same amount of time it takes to simply cook the pasta alone. But you can! This recipe packs huge flavor, too, so don't tell anyone it took less than 20 minutes to make this tasty meal.

⇨ This is a fantastic meal to make with kids. It's easy and fun for them to break up the pasta. And, while supervised by an adult, they can add all the ingredients to the pot themselves. Make mealtime not just about the meal, but about a memory!

To reduce cross-contamination use cutting boards, towels, utensils, and dish sponges dedicated for allergen-free cooking.

✓	GLUTEN
✓	WHEAT
✓	DAIRY
✓	CASEIN
⊘	EGG
⊘	NUT
✓	CORN
✓	SOY

'Be'
Traditional
Recipe

SERVES
4

TIME REQUIRED
55 min
(25 prep + 30 cooking)

2 tbsp butter

2 tbsp olive oil

4 green onions, chopped

8 baby carrots, chopped

2 garlic cloves, chopped

3 cups chicken stock

2 pinches saffron threads

1 cup orzo

¼ cup Parmesan cheese

dash cayenne pepper

Saffron Risotto

In a large pot, add the butter and oil over medium heat. Once the butter melts, add onions, carrots, and garlic. Mix well and cook about 5-8 minutes or until tender. Do not brown.

Add the orzo pasta and stir well for about 1 minute.

Add the chicken stock and bring to a boil. Reduce heat to low, just high enough for a soft simmer. Add the saffron and stir well.

Cook the orzo based on package instructions, or until done.

(If you cook your orzo too fast or it gets a bit dry, just add more stock or water.)

Once the orzo is done, add the Parmesan cheese and stir well. Add cayenne pepper if you want a little kick. Top with more Parmesan cheese to taste.

TIPS

⇨ Orzo is so much faster to cook than Arborio rice. I use this as my go-to risotto choice when I am short on time.

⇨ Saffron is expensive! So if you want to economize or are simply out of saffron, use turmeric instead. You get all the color and a hint of flavor for a lot less money.

64

'Free'
Allergen-free
Recipe

SERVES
4

TIME REQUIRED
60 min
(10 prep + 50 cooking)

⊘	GLUTEN
⊘	WHEAT
⊘	DAIRY
⊘	CASEIN
⊘	EGG
⊘	NUT
⊘	CORN
⊘	SOY

Read all food labels carefully and choose only products that are free of unwanted allergens for use in this recipe.

2½ cups mushrooms, sliced

1 cup of water

6 tbsp olive oil, divided:
  3 tbsp for mushrooms
  3 tbsp for rice sauté

4 cloves garlic, chopped

3 tbsp parsley, finely chopped

¼ tsp salt plus a few dashes

½ cup yellow onion, chopped

1 cup Arborio rice

32 oz organic, allergen-free, chicken stock

Mushroom Risotto

MUSHROOM TOPPING: In a medium sized pot, add the mushrooms and cup of water and bring to a boil. Boil for 3-4 minutes, stirring constantly. It will foam a bit during the boil, so keep stirring. Once the time is up, drain the mushrooms and rinse under cold water to stop the cooking process.

Add olive oil to the same pot over medium heat. Add chopped garlic and cook for 3 minutes. Add parsley and a dash of salt, and stir well. Return the mushrooms to the pot and cook over medium heat for 3 minutes.

Reduce heat to low, cover, and keep warm on the stove until the risotto is done cooking.

RISOTTO: In a large pot, add 3 tbsp of olive oil. Add the onion and cook several minutes until tender. Add the rice and stir well. Toast the rice for several minutes.

One cup at a time, add the stock to the rice. Cook the rice slowly, on low, and only add the next cup of stock once the previous cup has fully been absorbed by the rice. Don't try and speed up this process by using higher heat. Slow and steady wins the race with risotto!

Once all of the stock has been added and absorbed, taste the rice to check that it is fully cooked. If you need more liquid add either more stock or water.

When the risotto is done, place a scoop on a plate, top with mushrooms, and enjoy.

TIPS

⇒ Blanching the mushrooms before sautéing makes a huge difference in both flavor and texture. They lose their natural liquid yet absorb all that olive oil-garlic goodness.

⇒ If you are short on time, this recipe also works great with white rice... which takes half of the time.

BUTTERNUT SQUASH PASTA

'Be'
Traditional
Recipe

✓	GLUTEN
✓	WHEAT
✓	DAIRY
✓	CASEIN
✓	EGG
⊘	NUT
✓	CORN
⊘	SOY

SERVES
8

TIME REQUIRED
75 min
(30 prep + 45 cooking)

3 lbs butternut squash,
    seeded and halved

10 tbsp butter, divided:
    2 tbsp for filling
    8 tbsp for sauce

2 oz mascarpone cheese

¼ tsp plus a pinch salt

½ cup olive oil (for frying)

½ oz sage, cleaned, dry,
    leaves only

12 oz square won ton wrappers

TIPS

⇒ Use the reserved sage oil to
make your own salad dressing.

⇒ This recipe is for my sister Kelly
who helped me perfect it over
the years. Thanks, Kelly! ♡

Butternut Squash Pasta

FILLING: Place the cleaned butternut squash in a microwave safe dish and microwave for 10 minutes, or bake for about 30-45 minutes, until completely soft. Once totally soft, scoop out flesh and mash completely until smooth. Add 2 tbsp butter and mascarpone cheese and stir together. Add ¼ tsp salt and stir. This is the filling. Set aside.

WON TONS: In a cast iron skillet or non-stick pan, add olive oil over medium-heat. Add the sage leaves a few at a time without over-crowding. Let them fry until they start to release their fragrance and crisp a little (about 3 minutes). They burn quickly, so make sure they come out of the oil before they turn brown. Add a sprinkle of salt to the fried sage once it finishes frying. Repeat with several batches until the leaves are all fried. Reserve the oil for other uses. Lay one won ton wrapper out and place one teaspoon of filling in the center. Fill a glass with water. Wet your index finger and run it along the edge of the wrapper. This acts like glue. Grab opposite corners and connect, then grab the remaining opposite corners and connect to make a pyramid. Alternately, lay one won ton down, wet edges with water, add teaspoon of filling, and lay on top another won ton wrapper. Press hard on edges to seal. Repeat the process until all the filling or wrappers are used. Boil in large stock pot of salted water. When they float, they are done (about 4 minutes).

SAUCE: Bring a cube of butter to a boil in a small sauce pan. Stir constantly. It will foam up right before it browns. Once it browns, take it off the heat immediately. You want browned butter, not burned butter.

Now assemble your fabulous ravioli pasta. Place several cooked ravioli pasta on a plate. Spoon browned butter over it, and top with fried sage. Heaven!

66

SPAGHETTI SQUASH PASTA

'Free'
Allergen-free
Recipe

SERVES
3-4

TIME REQUIRED
75 min
(15 prep + 60 cooking)

⊘	GLUTEN
⊘	WHEAT
⊘	DAIRY
⊘	CASEIN
⊘	EGG
⊘	NUT
⊘	CORN
⊘	SOY

Read all food labels carefully and choose only products that are free of unwanted allergens for use in this recipe.

4 lbs spaghetti squash

2 tbsp water

2 tbsp olive oil

½ yellow onion, chopped

3 cloves garlic, chopped

¼ tsp salt

cayenne pepper to taste

2 cups tomatoes,
   seeded and chopped

14 oz can tomato sauce

¼ cup fresh basil, chopped

Spaghetti Squash Pasta

Preheat the oven to 375 degrees.

Cut the spaghetti squash in half lengthwise and remove seeds. Place in a large, foil covered roasting pan, cut-side down. Add 2 tbsp of water to the bottom to help increase the steam. Roast for 60 minutes, or until you can easily pierce the skin with a knife.

In a large pan, add olive oil over medium heat. Sauté onions and garlic until very tender. Add salt and cayenne pepper. Add chopped tomatoes, tomato sauce, and basil and simmer for 30 minutes on medium low. The longer the sauce cooks, the more the flavor develops.

Once the squash is cooked, gently scrape away the inside flesh with a fork into a bowl. If you want to serve the squash inside the skin, be careful not to scrape away too much flesh or pierce the skin. This will help the squash to keep its shape and not collapse.

Once all of the squash flesh is in a bowl, pour all of the sauce onto it. Mix gently so the sauce gets fully incorporated. Serve in separate bowls or right inside the squash for a delicious and beautiful meal.

TIP

⇒ This is an easy way to still feel like you're eating spaghetti - but without the carbs! The health benefits are amazing, too, with the squash providing lots of antioxidants and vitamin C and fiber.

SUNDRIED PESTO PASTA

'Be'
Traditional
Recipe

SERVES
4

TIME REQUIRED
25 min
(20 prep + 5 cooking)

½ cup parsley

1 cup packed basil leaves

¼ cup pine nuts

2 cloves garlic

¼ cup sundried tomatoes,
    oil packed

½ cup Parmesan cheese,
    shredded

½ tsp pepper

1 tsp salt

⅓ cup olive oil

17 oz potato gnocchi

Sundried Pesto Pasta

SAUCE: In a blender or food processor, add parsley, basil, pine nuts, garlic, sundried tomatoes, Parmesan cheese, pepper, and salt. Pulse for 5 seconds several times to blend. On low speed, add the oil a little at a time. Keep blending until all the oil is incorporated and all the ingredients have come together. Set the sauce aside.

Cook gnocchi according to the directions on the package. Once they are done, drain well and place into a large serving bowl.

While the gnocchi are warm, add about half of the pesto sauce and toss to combine. Additional sauce can be added based on each person's taste.

TIP

⇨ There is extra pesto sauce when you make this...unless you are at my house. I generally eat about half of it with French bread while the gnocchi are cooking. If you have more will-power than I, you could save the rest to use as a dip, or freeze for later use.

68

'Free'
Allergen-free Recipe

SERVES
3-4

TIME REQUIRED
30 min
(10 prep + 20 cooking)

⊘	GLUTEN
⊘	WHEAT
⊘	DAIRY
⊘	CASEIN
⊘	EGG
⊘	NUT
⊘	CORN
⊘	SOY

Read all food labels carefully and choose only products that are free of unwanted allergens for use in this recipe.

8 oz allergen-free pasta

3 tbsp olive oil

½ cup onion, chopped

2 cloves garlic, chopped

½ cup celery, chopped

1 cup cherry tomatoes, halved

½ cup basil, chopped

1 can cannellini beans,
   drained and rinsed

½ tsp salt

pepper to taste

Pesto Pasta

Bring a pot of water to boil and cook the pasta according to package directions.

In a separate pan, add olive oil over medium heat and sauté onions, garlic, and celery until tender. Add tomatoes and cook for 5 more minutes.

Add the basil and beans and stir well. Add salt and pepper to taste. Cover, reduce heat to medium low, and simmer for 5-10 more minutes.

Drain the pasta well after it finishes cooking. Separate the pasta into individual servings, top with the pesto bean sauce and serve.

(I looked everywhere to find packaged gnocchi that was allergen-free to be the "free" complement of this dish. Although gnocchi are made from potatoes, the packaged varieties are full of egg, soy, and wheat. After some thought, the white cannellini beans came to mind. The smooth and creamy texture of the bean reminds me a lot of gnocchi.)

TIPS

⇒ Cannellini beans are low in fat and high in fiber and protein. This recipe is tasty and so good for you!

⇒ The 3 servings will have more beans than pasta. If you prefer more pasta than beans, just double the pasta and keep the rest of the recipe the same.

PINE NUT PRIMAVERA

'Be'
Traditional
Recipe

SERVES
6

TIME REQUIRED
60 min
(45 prep + 15 cooking)

MAIN DISH

3 long carrots, cut in thirds

6-8 asparagus spears, cut in
thirds

1 red bell pepper, sliced

16 oz fettuccine pasta

2 tbsp butter

1 cup onion, chopped

1 cup white wine

1 cup chicken stock

Parmesan cheese, garnish

DRESSING

1½ cups packed basil leaves

½ cup pine nuts

½ cup extra virgin olive oil

1 tsp salt

2 cloves garlic, pressed

cayenne pepper to taste

TIP

⇒ This pasta is best when the
vegetables are fresh. Visit your
local farmer's market for the
best and ripest vegetables!

Pine Nut Primavera

DRESSING: Add basil, pine nuts, olive oil, salt, and garlic into a blender. Blend on low for a minute or until all of the ingredients have come together. Pour into a small dish and set aside.

PASTA: In a large stock pot, bring water to a boil. Blanch (boil) the carrots, asparagus, and bell pepper in the hot water for about 7 minutes. After the vegetables are blanched, remove the vegetables from the water (keep this water to use for the pasta), and rinse under cold water to stop the cooking process. Set the vegetables aside.

Return the water you used to blanch the vegetables back to the same pot and bring it to a boil. Cook the pasta according to instructions.

While the water comes back to a boil, add butter to a large sauté pan over medium heat. Once the butter has melted, add the onions and sauté for just a few minutes (do not brown). Once the onions become tender, add wine and bring to a boil. Let this boil gently for about 2-3 minutes to burn off most of the alcohol in the wine.

Add chicken stock and stir well. Once it comes to a boil, add all the vegetables and stir.

Once the pasta is done, drain it well and add it into the large sauté pan with the vegetables.

To serve, arrange one serving of the pasta and vegetables in a bowl. Top with a generous spoonful of the basil dressing and Parmesan cheese.

'Free'
Allergen-free
Recipe

SERVES
4

TIME REQUIRED
40 min
(10 prep + 30 cooking)

⊘ GLUTEN
⊘ WHEAT
⊘ DAIRY
⊘ CASEIN
⊘ EGG
⊘ NUT
⊘ CORN
⊘ SOY

*Read all food labels carefully and choose
only products that are free of unwanted
allergens for use in this recipe.*

8 oz allergen-free fettuccine

8 asparagus stalks, chopped into
    1 inch segments

1 red bell pepper, quartered

3 long carrots

5 tbsp olive oil, divided:
    2 tbsp to coat vegetables
    2 tbsp to sauté onions
    1 tbsp to toss with pasta

½ tsp allergen-free garlic powder

salt and pepper to taste

½ cup yellow onion, chopped

1 cup snow peas

TIP

⇨ This dish is so easy to make and
   all of the ingredients are so easy
   to find.

Garden Primavera

Bring a pot of water to boil and cook pasta accoring to package instructions.

In a large dish, add asparagus, bell pepper, and carrots. Add 2 tbsp olive oil, garlic powder, and dash of salt. Mix well to coat.

Heat the barbecue to medium. Add the asparagus, carrots, and bell peppers and cook until desired firmness. The carrots and peppers take the longest, so leave them on about 3 minutes or so more than the asparagus. Once they are cooked, chop the vegetables and add back to the dish and mix again with the seasonings.

(I know what you are thinking...do I really have to barbecue the vegetables? No, you don't, because you can roast all of these veggies in the oven, too. Personally, I'm a fan of getting outdoors and barbecuing, and the flavor that develops on the grill is just superb. If you can, give it a try. If you can't, roast them in the oven for 20 minutes at 400 degrees.)

In a sauté pan, add 2 tbsp olive oil over medium heat. Add onions and sauté for 3 minutes. Add snow peas and sauté for 3 minutes more.

Once the pasta is cooked and drained, place on a large serving platter or in a bowl. Add 1 tbsp olive oil and toss. Add the onions and snow peas and toss again. Add chopped and barbequed vegetables and toss once more. Serve and enjoy.

"Be"

CRISPY CHICKEN TENDERS

'Be'
Traditional
Recipe

SERVES
2-4

TIME REQUIRED
45 min
(25 prep + 20 cooking)

2 chicken breasts, sliced

2 eggs, beaten

1 cup Italian seasoned
    bread crumbs

½ tsp seasoned salt

½ tsp iodized or sea salt

1 tsp garlic powder

½ tsp pepper

1 cup olive oil (for frying)

TIPS

⇒ Forget eating out and try eating
   in for a change. Chicken strips
   are easy to make and are sure
   to please a hungry crowd.

⇒ Chicken strips are excellent
   with ranch dressing, BBQ sauce,
   honey mustard, or good
   old-fashioned ketchup.
   Mix it up and enjoy!

Crispy Chicken Tenders

Set up your work area like an assembly line. From left to right: plate of sliced chicken, bowl of beaten eggs, plate of bread crumbs, and an empty plate for coated chicken.

Season your sliced chicken with the seasoned salt, sea salt, garlic powder and pepper.

Start with one strip of chicken, coat it in the beaten egg mixture, then dredge in the bread crumbs until fully coated; set onto plate. Continue until all the pieces are coated.

In a large non-stick pan, add ½ cup of oil and bring to medium-high heat. Once the oil gets really hot add the chicken and reduce heat to medium. The chicken should sizzle right when it hits the oil.

Don't over-crowd the pan. Add only a few strips at a time. Turn the strips only once, after the outer edges have started to turn white.

Cook the other side until the chicken is cooked through and totally white at the center. Repeat with the rest of the chicken strips.

Since the bread crumbs burn easily, I generally change the oil half way. That ensures even cooking and no burned bits on the last batch of frying.

'Free'
Allergen-free
Recipe

SERVES
4

TIME REQUIRED
35 min
(10 prep + 25 cooking)

⊘	GLUTEN
⊘	WHEAT
⊘	DAIRY
⊘	CASEIN
⊘	EGG
⊘	NUT
⊘	CORN
⊘	SOY

Read all food labels carefully and choose only products that are free of unwanted allergens for use in this recipe.

2 cups Rice Chex™ brand cereal

16 oz organic chicken tenders

dashes salt, pepper
    and allergen-free
    garlic powder

4 tbsp olive oil

½ cup rice flour

Baked Chicken Tenders

Preheat oven to 400 degrees.

Add Rice Chex™ cereal to a blender or food processor and crush into fine crumbs. Pour onto a plate and set aside.

Rinse and drain chicken tenders, but do not pat dry. Season the chicken with salt, pepper and garlic powder.

Pour the olive oil onto a plate. Pour the rice flour onto a separate plate.

Set up your work area like an assembly line. From left to right: plate of seasoned chicken, plate of rice flour, plate with olive oil, plate with Chex™ crumbs and a lightly greased, large baking dish.

Start with one strip of chicken, coat it in the rice flour and then lightly cover with the olive oil on both sides. Next, dredge in the bread crumbs until fully coated, and place into the large baking dish. Continue until all the pieces are coated.

Bake in the oven for 20-25 minutes, or until fully cooked and golden brown.

TIPS

⇒ It's hard to believe that these chicken tenders are allergen-free. They look and taste like the traditional variety you buy at the supermarket or order in a restaurant. Making your own bread crumbs ensures that your crumbs are truly allergen-free. Plus it's very economical.

⇒ I prefer the light taste that you get when baking these tasty tenders in the oven. However, if you want a more robust chicken tender taste, fry them up in a pan or even deep fry.

CHICKEN CORDON BLEU

'Be'
Traditional Recipe

SERVES
2

TIME REQUIRED
55 min
(20 prep + 35 cooking)

¾ cup bread crumbs

2 organic chicken breasts

salt and pepper to taste

4 slices ham or prosciutto

4 slices Swiss cheese

3 tbsp butter, optional

TIPS

⇒ Chicken Cordon Bleu is a recipe that has grown in popularity since the 1960s—and rightfully so. Stuffing chicken with yummy slices of cheese and ham is a definite crowd pleaser.

⇒ If you don't like Swiss cheese, use any cheese you like. If you don't have ham or prosciutto, use bacon. Anything goes for this dish, so use what you love, or whatever's in your fridge.

⇒ My hubby, Lonnie, is the one who inspired the non-traditional addition of melted butter. If you want to shift flavor into overdrive, don't skip this step.

Chicken Cordon Bleu

Preheat the oven to 375 degrees.

Pour the bread crumbs into a bowl and set aside.

Lay one chicken breast on a cutting board and cover with a sheet of wax paper. Pound the chicken breast with a mallet until it is about ¼ inch thick. Repeat with second chicken breast. Season each with salt and pepper to taste.

To fill the chicken breast, lay one breast out and top with 2 slices of ham and 2 slices of Swiss cheese. Roll the chicken breast closed by starting at one end and firmly rolling until all the cheese and ham are completely enclosed.

Carefully place the rolled chicken into the bowl of bread crumbs. Press the crumbs into the chicken breast, both top and bottom. Repeat with second chicken breast. The chicken should be moist enough to have the bread crumbs stick. If you find you need more moisture, brush the chicken with a little water.

Place both chicken breasts into a baking dish.

As an optional step, melt 3 tbsp of butter and pour over the top of each breast.

Bake until completely cooked, 30-35 minutes. Don't overcook as the chicken will get dry.

'Free'
Allergen-free
Recipe

SERVES
2

TIME REQUIRED
54 min
(15 prep + 39 cooking)

⊘ GLUTEN
⊘ WHEAT
⊘ DAIRY
⊘ CASEIN
⊘ EGG
⊘ NUT
⊘ CORN
⊘ SOY

Read all food labels carefully and choose only products that are free of unwanted allergens for use in this recipe.

2 cups Rice Chex™ brand mix

3 tbsp olive oil, divided
    2 tbsp for Chex™ coating
    1 tbsp for onions

½ tsp fresh rosemary,
    chopped fine

salt and pepper to taste

½ cup yellow onion, chopped

2 organic chicken breasts

2 slices ham or prosciutto

Chicken Cordon New

Preheat the oven to 375 degrees.

Line a cookie sheet with aluminum foil. Spread out Rice Chex cereal. Add 2 tbsp olive oil, chopped rosemary and salt to taste. Mix gently. Brown in the oven for 3-4 minutes, stirring every minute. Watch closely as the Rice Chex can burn easily at this temperature. Once the cereal starts to brown, remove from the oven and cool. Once cool, blend in a blender or food processor until you have fine crumbs. Add crumbs to a bowl and set aside.

In a pan, add 1 tbsp olive oil over medium heat and sauté onions until they become soft and slightly brown. Add salt and pepper to taste. Remove from heat and set aside.

Lay one chicken breast on a cutting board. Cover the chicken with a sheet of wax paper. and pound with a mallet until it is about ¼ inch thick. Repeat with second chicken breast. Season each with salt and pepper to taste.

To fill the chicken breast, lay one breast out and top with 2 slices of ham and half of the sautéed onions. Roll the chicken breast closed, rolling until all the onions and ham are completely enclosed.

Carefully place the rolled chicken into the bowl of crumbs. Press the crumbs into the chicken breast, both top and bottom. Repeat with second chicken breast. The chicken should be moist enough for the crumbs. If you find you need more moisture, brush the chicken with a little water before adding crumbs.

Place both chicken breasts into a baking dish. Bake until completely cooked, about 30-35 minutes. Don't overcook as the chicken will get dry.

TIP

⇨ Allergy-free doesn't have to mean
   taste-free. This recipe adds bold
   flavor without any allergens.
   So easy to make and so tasty.
   Hooray for Chicken Cordon New!

✓	GLUTEN
✓	WHEAT
✓	DAIRY
✓	CASEIN
⊘	EGG
⊘	NUT
✓	CORN
✓	SOY

'Be'
Traditional
Recipe

SERVES
2

TIME REQUIRED
30 min
(15 prep + 15 cooking)

3 tbsp lime juice, divided:
    2 tbsp for marinade
    1 tbsp for dressing

1 tsp cumin

salt and pepper

1 uncooked chicken breast,
    chopped

1 tbsp olive oil

2 tbsp sour cream

2 tbsp cilantro, chopped

2 soft flour tortillas

¼ cup grated cotija cheese

¼ cup lettuce, shredded

¼ cup tomatoes, chopped

¼ cup onions, chopped

TIPS

⇒ If you are short on time, you can buy cooked chicken.

⇒ This recipe is a great choice when you have to feed a crowd. You can prep all the ingredients ahead of time and assemble quickly once you are ready.

Chicken Tacos

MARINADE: Combine 2 tbsp lime juice, 1 tsp cumin, and dashes of salt and pepper to taste in a small container. Mix well. Pour the marinade over the chopped raw chicken breast and mix well to coat all of the pieces.

In a medium sized pan, add olive oil and sauté the chicken over medium heat until completely cooked. This will take 5-10 minutes.

Once the chicken is cooked, remove from heat, place on a plate and cover with aluminum foil. Let the chicken rest for 5 minutes. This step will keep the chicken moist.

DRESSING: Combine sour cream, chopped cilantro, 1 tbsp lime juice and a dash of salt. Mix well.

To assemble the tacos, take one flour tortilla and spread half of the sour cream dressing on one half of the tortilla to the center. Add half of the chopped chicken, cotija cheese, lettuce, tomatoes and onions.
Fold over and serve.

'Free'
Allergen-free
Recipe

SERVES
2

TIME REQUIRED
30 min
(15 prep + 15 cooking)

⊘	GLUTEN
⊘	WHEAT
⊘	DAIRY
⊘	CASEIN
⊘	EGG
⊘	NUT
⊘	CORN
⊘	SOY

Read all food labels carefully and choose only products that are free of unwanted allergens for use in this recipe.

¾ cup orange juice

4 tbsp fresh lime juice, divided:
    3 tbsp for glaze
    1 tbsp for salsa

1 tsp cumin

dash chipotle chili pepper

1 uncooked, organic chicken
    breast, chopped

1 tsp olive oil

salt and pepper to taste

½ cup tomatoes, chopped

2 tbsp onions, chopped

1 tbsp cilantro, chopped

2 large lettuce leaves

½ avocado, cubed

Lettuce Wraps

ORANGE GLAZE: In a small pot, add orange juice, 3 tbsp of lime juice, cumin and dash of chipotle chili pepper and reduce over medium heat until the liquid turns into a syrup or thick glaze.

While the liquid is reducing, sauté the chopped chicken in a pan over medium heat with olive oil until cooked through. Add salt and pepper to taste while cooking.

Once the chicken is cooked and once the reduction is done, add the cooked chicken into the pan with the orange glaze and mix well to incorporate. Remove from heat, place on a plate, and cover with aluminum foil. Let the chicken rest for 5 minutes. This step keeps the chicken moist.

SALSA: Combine tomatoes, onions, cilantro and 1 tbsp of lime juice and mix well. Add salt to taste.

To assemble, take one lettuce leaf, and add half of the chicken, salsa and avocados. Repeat for the second portion.

TIP

⇒ You can buy and toast allergen-free tortillas if you would prefer that over a lettuce leaf. However, if you are looking for something a little lighter and carbohydrate free, the lettuce leaf is worth a try.

✓	GLUTEN
✓	WHEAT
⊘	DAIRY
⊘	CASEIN
✓	EGG
✓	NUT
✓	CORN
✓	SOY

'Be'
Traditional
Recipe

SERVES
4

TIME REQUIRED
10 min
(10 prep + 0 cooking)

2 cups cooked chicken,
    shredded or chopped

3 stalks celery, chopped

¼ cup walnuts, chopped

¼ cup red onion, chopped

½ cup mayonnaise

½ tsp celery salt

pepper to taste

4 slices sourdough or
    French bread

TIPS

⇒ Cooked chicken is so easy to find
    in the supermarket and makes
    this chicken salad fast, fresh
    and delicious.

⇒ The ingredients in this recipe are
    very basic. Go ahead and add
    more or less of the ingredients
    to suit your taste. Add additional
    ingredients, too, if you want to
    switch it into high gear. Maybe
    a little chopped Anaheim chili
    for some spice or even some
    grapes for some sweet. Have fun
    playing with your food!

Classic Chicken Salad

In a large bowl combine chopped chicken, celery, walnuts and onion.
Mix well.

Add mayonnaise and celery salt and mix again.

Add salt and pepper to taste.

Spoon half of the mixture onto a slice of bread. Top with the other slice to
make a sandwich. Cut in half to serve. Repeat this process for the second
chicken salad sandwich.

CHICKEN AND APPLE SALAD

⊘	GLUTEN
⊘	WHEAT
⊘	DAIRY
⊘	CASEIN
⊘	EGG
⊘	NUT
⊘	CORN
⊘	SOY

'Free'
Allergen-free
Recipe

SERVES
4

TIME REQUIRED
10 min
(10 prep + 0 cooking)

Read all food labels carefully and choose only products that are free of unwanted allergens for use in this recipe.

MAIN

½ cup chopped green apple

1 tsp lemon juice

2 cups allergen-free, organic cooked chicken, chopped or shredded

2 stalks celery, chopped

2 green onions, chopped

¼ cup parsley, chopped

½ red bell pepper, chopped fine

DRESSING

1 cup canned garbanzo beans, rinsed

6 tbsp water

8 tbsp lemon juice

½ tsp salt

½ tsp pepper

6 tbsp olive oil

TIP

⇒ Since this recipe doesn't have mayonnaise, you not only avoid allergens, but you save on fat and calories too!

Chicken and Apple Salad

When chopping the apple, be sure to add lemon juice to it so it slows the browning that happens once the apple is cut.

DRESSING: Combine garbanzo beans, water, lemon juice, salt and pepper in a blender. Blend on low until it becomes smooth. Slowly add in the olive oil and blend until it is incorporated.

In a large bowl, combine the chopped chicken, celery, onions, parsley, bell pepper and apple. Mix gently.

Add the dressing and mix wel. Serve and enjoy.

(This is an awesome recipe to take to a picnic, party or any gathering. Simply mix all your ingredients EXCEPT the dressing, and package it up well. Once you get to your event, add the dressing and serve. If you can't find organic, allergen-free cooked chicken, play it safe and cook it yourself.)

✓	GLUTEN
✓	WHEAT
⊘	DAIRY
⊘	CASEIN
⊘	EGG
⊘	NUT
⊘	CORN
⊘	SOY

COUNTRY CHICKEN CACCIATORE

'Be'
Traditional Recipe

SERVES
4-6

TIME REQUIRED
55 min
(15 prep + 40 cooking)

1½ cups unbleached white flour,
    divided

4-5 chicken breasts,
    cubed into 1-inch chunks

1 cup water

½ cup olive oil (more if needed)

½ cup onion, chopped

3 celery stalks, sliced

3 garlic cloves, chopped

8 oz can tomato sauce

¼ tsp allspice

2 tbsp sugar

½ tsp salt

½ tsp black pepper

1 tbsp parsley, chopped

4 oz canned mushrooms

TIPS

⇒ If you want a "soupier" version, add 14.5 oz of canned chopped tomatoes.

⇒ Frying up the chicken takes time, so if you want a short-cut, buy cooked chicken. It's not the same flavor and texture, but it will still be delicious.

Country Chicken Cacciatore

In a large zip-top bag, add 1 cup flour and cubed chicken pieces. Shake until all the pieces are coated. Add more flour if necessary.

In a small bowl, combine remaining flour and water and stir well. Set aside.

In a large pot, heat oil over medium heat and fry the chicken. Brown it slightly to add flavor. Work in small batches and don't overcrowd the pan. Turn the chicken pieces, and when they are golden brown on each side, remove and set aside. The chicken does not need to be cooked through because it will cook for 30 more minutes in the sauce you will prepare. If the oil gets dark from burned bits of flour, start over with a new batch of oil. Browned bits of flour are good but burned is not! Remove all chicken and set aside on a plate.

In the same oil you fried the chicken, add onions, celery and garlic. Sauté for a few minutes until they become translucent.

Add the water/flour mixture to the pan and mix well. This will thicken your dish. Scrape the browned bits at the bottom for added flavor.

Add the tomato sauce, allspice, sugar, salt, pepper, parsley and mushrooms.

Add the golden fried chicken and simmer for 30 minutes.

'Free'
Allergen-free Recipe

SERVES
4-6

TIME REQUIRED
65 min
(15 prep + 50 cooking)

⊘ GLUTEN
⊘ WHEAT
⊘ DAIRY
⊘ CASEIN
⊘ EGG
⊘ NUT
⊘ CORN
⊘ SOY

Read all food labels carefully and choose only products that are free of unwanted allergens for use in this recipe.

8 organic chicken thighs, skin on

salt and pepper

4 tbsp olive oil

1 cup chopped carrot

1 cup chopped celery

1 cup chopped onion

1 cup chopped red bell pepper

3 cloves garlic, chopped

2 cups grape tomatoes, halved

8 oz can tomato sauce

Bruno's Cacciatore

Season both sides of the chicken thighs with salt and pepper.

In a large pan, add olive oil, bring to high heat and brown the chicken thighs. Don't overcrowd the pan as it will steam the chicken instead of brown it. Once the chicken thighs are browned on both sides, remove from heat and set aside.

In the same pan with the remaining oil from the fried chicken, add the chopped carrot, celery, onion and red bell pepper. Sauté for 10 minutes over medium heat.

Add chopped tomatoes and tomato sauce. Mix well to combine.

Transfer each chicken thigh into the pan and nestle into the sauce. Cook, covered for 30 minutes at a soft simmer. Turn each thigh over after 15 minutes. Serve hot right from the pan.

TIP

⇒ This chicken was my sister Julie's favorite because it reminded her of the way my Dad liked to make it. The large pieces of chicken with the skin on adds so much flavor. If you don't like thighs, use drumsticks, or even chicken breasts.

✓	GLUTEN
✓	WHEAT
✓	DAIRY
✓	CASEIN
⊘	EGG
⊘	NUT
✓	CORN
✓	SOY

'Be'
Traditional
Recipe

SERVES
2

TIME REQUIRED
20 min
(10 prep + 10 cooking)

1 grilled or baked chicken breast

½ cup artichoke hearts,
    drained and chopped

½ cup Kalamata olives, chopped

4 oz chevre or goat cheese

dash black pepper

2 tsp real butter

4 slices sourdough or French
    bread

2 large roasted red bell peppers

10-12 spinach leaves

TIP

⇒ Panini presses are awesome! Get one if you can. If you don't have one, you can still make this recipe. Toast your bread in a toaster oven, rub butter on one side of each bread slice, and assemble. If you want to get really fancy, check out Alton Brown's suggestions for paninis without the press. His techniques never cease to amaze me.

Savory Chicken Panini

Preheat a panini press.

Slice the grilled or baked chicken breast into strips.

Combine the chopped artichoke hearts, Kalamata olives, chevre or goat cheese and dash of pepper and mix well.

Rub butter on only one side of each piece of bread. Place the ingredients on the non-buttered side of the bread. First add half of the cheese spread, one roasted bell pepper, half of the chicken strips and half of the spinach leaves. Put the other half of the bread on top with the buttered side up so it touches the grill.

Grill your panini until the grill marks on the bread are golden brown.

Repeat the steps for the second panini sandwich.

'Free'
Allergen-free Recipe

SERVES
2

TIME REQUIRED
25 min
(10 prep + 15 cooking)

⊘	GLUTEN
⊘	WHEAT
⊘	DAIRY
⊘	CASEIN
⊘	EGG
⊘	NUT
⊘	CORN
⊘	SOY

Read all food labels carefully and choose only products that are free of unwanted allergens for use in this recipe.

¼ cup basil leaves, chopped

4 tbsp olive oil, divided:
   3 tbsp for spread
   1 tbsp for sauté

dashes garlic powder,
   salt and black pepper

½ cup yellow onion, sliced

1 grilled or baked organic
   chicken breast

4 slices allergen-free brown rice
   bread

Pesto Chicken Panini

Preheat a panini press.

SPREAD: Combine the finely chopped basil leaves, 3 tbsp olive oil, dash of garlic powder, salt and black pepper and mix well. Set aside.

In a sauté pan, add 1 tbsp olive oil over medium heat. Add sliced onions and a dash of salt, and sauté until the onions are golden in color. Once they are done, remove from heat and set aside.

Slice the grilled or baked chicken breast into strips.

To assemble, top one slice of bread with half of the basil spread, chicken, and sautéed onions. Cover with another slice of bread and toast in your panini press until golden brown.

Repeat the steps for the second panini sandwich.

TIPS

⇒ The fresh basil pesto boosts the complexity of flavors in this dish so nicely. I always double the basil pesto because I can never seem to get enough.

⇒ If you don't have a panini press, no problem – simply toast the bread in your toaster. Just make sure you throughly clean the toaster first, to keep your panini absolutely gluten-free.

www.befreecooking.blogspot.com — *To reduce cross-contamination use cutting boards, towels, utensils, and dish sponges dedicated for allergen-free cooking.*

85

⊘	GLUTEN
⊘	WHEAT
✓	DAIRY
✓	CASEIN
⊘	EGG
⊘	NUT
⊘	CORN
⊘	SOY

'Be'
Traditional
Recipe

SERVES
4

TIME REQUIRED
55 min
(10 prep + 45 cooking)

parchment or wax paper

4 chicken breasts, skinless

dashes black pepper and
    cayenne pepper

4 tbsp parsley, chopped

4 slices prosciutto

4 cheese sticks, Monterey jack

4 tbsp butter

salt

toothpicks

TIPS

⇒ The minimal amount of butter
and the natural juices from
the chicken make for the most
wonderful sauce. The chicken will
be tender and salted perfectly
from the prosciutto. This is a
fantastic dinner party main
course.

⇒ This dish was inspired by the leftover cheese sticks and deli meat
I inevitably have in my fridge.
Hopefully this will inspire you to
use those leftovers from your own
fridge!

Prosciutto Stuffed Chicken

Preheat the oven to 350 degrees.

Drape a piece of wax or parchment paper over one chicken breast and pound with a mallet until it is 1 inch thick. Repeat process with each additional chicken breast.

Take one pounded chicken breast and lay it flat. Sprinkle with black pepper, cayenne pepper and 1 tbsp of parsley. In the center of the breast add 1 slice prosciutto, 1 cheese stick and 1 tbsp butter.

Roll the chicken breast until all the cheese and prosciutto are completely enclosed. Spear with toothpicks to keep in place.

Add additional pepper and salt on the top, to taste. Repeat with the remaining breasts.

Bake in a large casserole dish covered with foil for 35-45 minutes or until completely cooked.

When serving, plate each breast and ladle a spoonful of the juice from the baking pan on top for added flavor. Slice or keep whole for serving.

86

ARTICHOKE STUFFED CHICKEN

'Free'
Allergen-free Recipe

SERVES
2

TIME REQUIRED
55 min
(20 prep + 35 cooking)

⊘ GLUTEN
⊘ WHEAT
⊘ DAIRY
⊘ CASEIN
⊘ EGG
⊘ NUT
⊘ CORN
⊘ SOY

Read all food labels carefully and choose only products that are free of unwanted allergens for use in this recipe.

4 slices of bacon

parchment or wax paper

4 organic chicken breasts

4 tbsp fresh lemon juice

salt and pepper

8 oz can artichoke hearts, drained and chopped

¼ cup arugula lettuce

2 tbsp reserved bacon drippings

Artichoke Stuffed Chicken

Preheat the oven to 350 degrees.

In a large sauté pan, cook bacon over medium heat until completely cooked. Set aside and crumble once cool. Reserve the bacon drippings.

Drape a piece of wax or parchment paper over one chicken breast and pound with a mallet until it is 1 inch thick. Repeat process with the each additional chicken breast.

Take one pounded chicken breast and lay it flat. Pour 1 tbsp fresh lemon juice over the chicken. Sprinkle with salt and black pepper to taste. In the center of the breast add ¼ each of the chopped artichoke hearts, arugula lettuce and crispy bacon.

Roll the chicken breast closed by starting at one end and firmly rolling until all the bacon, artichoke hearts and arugula are enclosed. Spear with toothpicks to keep in place. Repeat with the remaining breasts.

Place the rolled chicken breasts in a casserole dish. Spoon the reserved bacon drippings over the tops of the rolled chicken breasts. Add additional pepper and salt to taste.

Bake covered with foil for 35-45 minutes or until completely cooked.

When serving, plate each breast and ladle a spoonful of the juice from the baking dish on the top for added flavor. Slice or keep whole for serving.

TIPS

⇒ Pounding a chicken breast and stuffing it with ingredients you love is a great and easy way to make a tasty dish. These are my favorite ingredients, but go ahead and explore by adding or substituting your own. Basil leaves and sundried tomatoes are a great combo, as is ham and jalapeños.

⇒ My sisters Lisa, Kelly, and Julie all love this dish. It's a favorite for us to make together.

87

SPICY POPPER STUFFED PEPPER

'Be'
Traditional
Recipe

SERVES
2

TIME REQUIRED
60 min
(10 prep + 50 cooking)

4 oz ground chicken

salt and pepper, to taste

1 jalapeño, seeded and diced

½ cup panko bread crumbs

4 oz cream cheese

2 oz Monterey jack cheese, grated

2 oz cheddar cheese, grated

2 large green bell peppers

TIPS

➪ I love the taste of a jalapeño popper, so I duplicated the yumminess of the mini version in a super-sized version. It's so cheesy and delicious.

➪ I really like my bell peppers to be soft and easy to cut with a fork, but if you prefer to have some crunch to your bell pepper, cook for only 25 minutes uncovered and 5 minutes covered.

➪ These peppers pack huge flavor. I especially love eating them as leftovers at breakfast. Yum yum!

Spicy Popper Stuffed Pepper

Preheat the oven to 400 degrees.

In a non-stick sauté pan, add ground chicken and dashes of salt and pepper to taste. Sauté over medium heat until completely cooked. Remove from heat and transfer to a medium-sized bowl.

To the cooked chicken, add the diced jalapeño, bread crumbs, cream cheese, Monterey jack cheese and cheddar cheese. Mix well to combine.

Clean the green bell peppers well by running them under cold water. Cut around the stem in a circular motion and pull upward. Once the top is off the pepper, gently remove any remaining fibers inside the pepper. To remove any additional seeds inside, fill the inside of the pepper with cold water and then pour out the water. Be careful not to split or crack your bell pepper.

Gently stuff the bell peppers with the chicken and cheese mixture and place them onto a baking dish.

Bake for 40 minutes uncovered to brown the top, then an additional 10 minutes covered with aluminum foil to fully melt the cheese.

Carefully transfer to a serving plate and enjoy.